DEFIANT
THRONE

ARIA MIRANDA

Paperback: 978-1-961438-70-5
eBook: 978-1-961438-71-2
Library of Congress Control Number: 2023915635

Ordering Information:

Prime Seven Media
518 Landmann St.
Tomah City, WI 54660

Printed in the United States of America

TABLE OF CONTENTS

Chapter 1: The Banquet 7

Chapter 2: The Decree 16

Chapter 3: The Warning..23

Chapter 4: The Advisors 30

Chapter 5: The City of Susa...38

Chapter 6: Girls, Girls, Girls 47

Chapter 7: The Mighty Greeks 58

Chapter 8: The Royal Harem 68

Chapter 9: Rumors of War 78

Chapter 10: A Newborn King... 87

Chapter 11: Marduk- God of Storms 96

Chapter 12: Amara 109

Chapter 13: The Throne Room.. 120

Chapter 14: Woo Me 127

Chapter 15: The Garden 135

Chapter 16: Who to Devour... 141

Chapter 17: The Arabs 151

Chapter 18: The Akitu Celebration 157

Chapter 19: Gaia 166

Chapter 20: Battle of Babylon 173

Chapter 21: Vengeance is Mine 182

Chapter 22: Accusations 192

Chapter 23: Pathways 214

Chapter 24: The Coronation 226

Chapter 25: Mobilization 236

Chapter 26: The Battle of Thermopylae 252

Chapter 27: Death has a sting. 262

Chapter 28: The Battle of Salamis 269

Chapter 29: The Defeat 287

Chapter 30: The Price 298

ACKNOWLEDGEMENTS

Dedicated to: Kayia Rose Tirado, Granddaughter
To my mother, Martha Bracero, who fully believed in me.

Mentors:
Fanstory Friends
Michael Sewall (Author)

Editor, book cover designer
Jane Davis Agent -Prime Seven Media

Contributors to the content
Rose Mary Sheldon-Academia.edu
Stavros Paspalas-Academia.edu
Plutarch, The Parallel Lives
Richard Stoneman (Author)

Academic content support
Iran Chamber Society
Pars Times

Organizations

University of Chicago Press- A.T. Olmstead -The History of the Persian Empire.

Hakin Abol Qasem Ferdowsi Tougi- Shahnameh the Epic of Kings

"I was just a boy when King Nebuchadnezzar besieged Jerusalem and was taken to Babylon. An army of Chaldeans, Syrians, Moabites, and Ammonites entered Jerusalem. They captured King Jehoiakim, the Queen, and plundered the treasures from the Temple of the Lord. The golden vessels King Solomon of Israel had placed in the temple were taken to Babylon. The city walls were razed, and the inhabitants were taken as exiles. I was given to the care of eunuchs, renamed Belteshazzar, and trained in the schools of the Chaldean."

Daniel looked up from the scroll he was writing on, took a deep breath, and continued:

"Nebuchadnezzar, King of the Babylonian Empire, was a strong warrior with significant military power, conquering many neighboring city-states. After his death, Nabonidus claimed the throne as the sole heir by conjuring up lies with the help of the army generals and the divinities of celestial phenomena, which favored him as the next King. He assigned his son Prince Belshazzar to run the day-to-day activities of the Empire in his absence. Meanwhile, he busied himself building temples for the moon God, Sin. The Babylonians worshiped many gods, but Marduk was the main deity.

This was the beginning of sorrow.

I remember when Zenia was born; she was a beautiful, spirited child—the apple of her father's eye. One day, Prince Belshazzar had a grand feast with wine, food, music, and celebration. He invited thousands of his officers to eat and drink freely. While lightheaded with wine, he remembered the gold and silver cups taken from the temple of Jerusalem and brought to Babylon. He was a pompous simpleton and ordered the sacred vessels to be brought to him. He, his army, and concubines used the sacred goblets of gold to drink to their idols.

As they toasted from the vessels, they saw a disembodied finger of a man writing on the wall. Belshazzar became pale with fear, and his knees knocked together with terror. He called for the magicians and astrologers to interpret the writing on the wall. None of them could understand or tell him what it meant. He grew increasingly hysterical with terror, and his officers were also frightened. I was called to interpret the writing, for it was said, 'I was full of wisdom and knowledge.' The King offered me up to half the kingdom, but what's that to an old man? I just wanted to go back to the land of my birth.

I stood before the King and spoke with authority, for I knew. God gave Nebuchadnezzar a kingdom and crowned him with the majesty that all the world's nations trembled before him in fear. He killed anyone who offended him and spared any he liked. At his whim, they rose and fell. When his heart and mind became hardened with pride, God removed him from his royal throne, and he became like an animal, eating grass like an ox, and his body became hairy like a wolf. You, Belshazzar, knew all this, yet you have not humbled yourself. You have defiled the Lord of Heaven and brought these goblets from his temple, and you and your officers, their wives, and the concubines have been drinking from them while praising the gods of SILVER...GOLD...BRASS...IRON...WOOD, and STONE! This is an oracle from God, the creator of Heaven and Earth. Mene, Tekel, Parsin. Mene means God has numbered the days of your reign, and they will be ended. Tekel means you have been weighed in God's balance and failed the test. Parsin means your kingdom is divided and given to the Medes and the Persians.

King Darius the Mede entered the city that same hour, killed Belshazzar, and captured the city. The kingdom was divided between the Medes and the Persians under the rule of King Cyrus.

Zenia was just a child when this occurred. During the mass confusion, she ran into Darius' arms, seeking protection, thinking it was her father because he was sitting on the throne. Darius held the scared child in his arms for a long time before she realized it was not her father. He felt compassion for the weeping young girl and would not harm her. Instead, he took her to the Susa Palace, where he raised her as his daughter."

CHAPTER ONE

THE BANQUET

King Dawit, the Exalted Shah, sat majestically on his gold and silver throne. His home, the Shushan Palace, was adorned, decorated, and ready for the banquet. He looked around at all the glory, power, and riches displayed for the honorary guest and thought of his greatness. The invites included his Officials, affluent representatives of the Persian and Media nobles, and princes. The one-hundred-and-sixty-day event was in preparation for a military campaign against Greece.

Queen Zenia, the wife of the Great King, also held a banquet hosting the royal women in spacious gardens of beautiful flowers, natural springs, and luscious greenery. The wives of officials roamed without shame, discarding their heavy wraps, unbound their hair, and ran around in their modesty. In the celebrations, abundant royal wine was served in golden goblets. The banquet tables were full of royal delicacies, including hummingbird tongues, heron eggs, and goose mousse.

After many days of drunkenness and debauchery, King Dawit called for Zenia to appear before him and his guests, wearing nothing more than her crown, for she was beauty to behold.

"Why would my husband make such a strange request?" she asked the messenger as she was quite perplexed. "The Shah delights in thy beauty, Queen Zenia, and he would like to share thy glory with his guests." The Queen could hardly believe her ears. She thought the King must be overcome with wine to make such an appalling request.

After the initial shock, Queen Zenia decided to reason with the King. "Deliver this personal message to the Shah. She wrote: "My beloved Shah, now, after many days of feasting, give ear unto my plea, and ask not that I do this which is evil in the sight of the honored guest."

King Dawit would not take no for an answer. "Go and get Zenia and bring her to me," he said, drunk. "She must obey."

"You are the King!" taunted one of the noble leaders, "Who runs this palace?" The other leaders joined in the taunting. Kaleb, an ambitious man who aspired to greatness, went to get Zenia.

Queen Zenia was the great-granddaughter of King Nebuchadnezzar of Babylon, King Amel-Marduk's granddaughter, and Prince Belshazzar's daughter. She was kidnapped after King Darius had brutally murdered her father and captured her country. The thought of what had happened to her during the past eight years was still fresh in her mind. Her blood boiled with fury every time she thought about it. When she was given as a bride to the Shah, she humbly accepted, for she had no choice but to wait to avenge her father's death quietly and restore the throne of Babylon.

"I am a Royal Queen!" Zenia cried in anger. The officials' wives were equally appalled. "Listen to my words, my sisters. I am not a goddess to be put on a platform, nor a concubine to be shown as a slave. Dare the King try to shame me and dishonor the name of my fathers. I will not display myself before a multitude of degenerates and inebriates."

"Indeed, the Shah must be influenced by daevas of wine, tempting him to do evil," said one of the women. They all agreed it was an unnatural demand, but no one dared to grumble against the King, for the wrath of the King was furious.

When Kaleb went to get the Queen, she slapped him with her slipper and had her tiger, Amber, chase him out of the garden. She sent a messenger with her final reply, for she could not hold her peace anymore. "You, son of my father's stable boy. My father drank wine in the assembly of thousands of people and did not get drunk, but you are senseless with wine. I will not defile myself before your guest."

The King was furious when Kaleb returned bleeding and reported what Zenia had done. "The Queen dares to refuse my orders," he slurred, pacing back and forth like a caged tiger. He called for his advisors, the seven nobles of Persia and Media, wise men who understood the laws and justice, Karshena, Shethar, Admatha, Tarshish, Meres, Marsena, and Memukan. These men were honored and respected in the kingdom and close to the King.

"What must I do to restore order in my palace?" he said. "The Queen has refused my orders. What advice do you give?" he asked, staggering.

"According to the laws, because she did not obey the command of the King, she has wronged not only the King but the princes and all the people who are in the kingdom's provinces," said Kaleb. He was a Hebrew exile who did not return to Jerusalem with his countrymen, for he had significant influence in Susa, thirsting for more. Gabe, the King's bodyguard, wondered why Kaleb added to the laws. The offense was on the King, not everyone else.

"Listen to me, my son," Mother Queen advised. "All the women in the dynasty will know about the Queen's intolerable behavior; they will despise, disobey, and give no respect to their husbands'. They will say among themselves, 'King Dawit sanctioned Queen Zenia to stand before him, and she refused.' This will create contempt and wrath throughout the kingdom if you do not correct her defiant behavior now.'"

Queen Mother never approved of the royal marriage. It was her late husband's idea to unite both countries and pacify the Babylonians, who had revolted consistently against the Persians. She should be one to judge, thought Gabe. Mother Queen ruled the empire and was more feared than the King. What was the old sorcerer up to now?

A eunuch suggested, "If it pleases the King, a decree can go forth out from him, to be recorded in the laws of the Persians and the Medes so that it will not be altered, to banish Queen Zenia from the presence of Your Highness." King Dawit did not hear the suggestion. He had fallen asleep in his drunkenness. Gabe took him to his sleeping chambers, but the royal decree was sealed with the King's signet ring and made official.

The King fell into a deep sleep, slumbering for many days. Queen Zenia herself was unaware of the decree. Yet, she found it peculiar; the King had not called her into his chambers; he usually called for her several nights a week unless he had an infirmity.

One day, the Queen heard the royal housekeeper, Rosie, conversing with the head eunuch. "The King has instructed us to go and find the most beautiful girls in the empire and bring them to him for his pleasures," said Rosie. "I will appoint messengers in each province to select young lovelies for the royal harem," said Haggai.

What's going on? The Queen wondered. Why was the King requesting to bring virgin lovelies to the royal harem? The royal harem had enough concubines and servants. She had limited the occupants of the harem to reduce expenses.

After the eunuch left the room, Zenia approached Rosie, who had been a royal aide for many years and knew more than she had led people to believe. She was known in the palace for dropping her ear to pick up information others were not privileged to. Zenia startled Rosie when she appeared from behind a curtain. "Your Majesty, I knew not that you were present," she said, stunned.

"Your black heart betrays you; hold not the truth from me, and tell me what I hear," the Queen demanded.

"Judge me not so hastily, Your Majesty; I fear I know not what you ask of me." Rosie lied.

"Dare you to try to beguile me with fables and lies? Sway from evil, and fall not into temptation against the Queen of Persia."

Rosie thought of telling Zenia the truth. She was no longer the Queen of Persia but banished, dethroned, and worthless. The royal servant, however, was wise and chose her words wisely. "My lady, show compassion on a dead dog like me. I humbly plead for your forgiveness, adored Queen of the Empire."

"Beguile me not. If you know not what I am asking, be on your way," Zenia replied, grabbing Rosie by the hair and tossing her out of the meeting hall. "May your cunningness find you," she laughed. Zenia knew Rosie was fearful, not so much for what she could do to her, but Mother Queen was cruel, even to her faithful servants.

Mother Queen was Cyrus the Great's eldest daughter and Darius the Great's wife. Her mother, Queen Cassandane, was the beloved wife of Cyrus, and he never stopped lamenting after her death. The Achaemenid Royal Queen had significant authority in the royal house. Her son, King Dawit, was not the eldest son of King Darius, but he was born after King Darius had ascended to the throne as King, vilifying him as the crown prince. There was no woman competitive to Mother Queen's noble status, until Zenia arrived at the harem. Mother Queen followed the teachings of Zarathustra. She wanted to reform Persia from polytheism into the highest god, Ahura Mazda, following the threefold oaths of good thoughts, good words, and good deeds. She believed in the cosmology of dualism, good and evil, where good will ultimately triumph over evil. Her teachings taught the free will to choose, the concept of judgment after death, paradise, a place of torment, benevolent spirits, and evil spirits called daevas. After the birth of her son, she was troubled by a lump on her breast, which the Royal Doctor removed. During this time, Rosie becomes the maidservant to the noblewoman. "Mother Queen will hear about this," said Rosie as she limped away.

CHAPTER TWO

THE DECREE

The King's decree spread throughout the land: "Hear ye, hear ye," announced a royal soldier; "King Dawit has decreed that all virgin lovelies from ages thirteen to twenty report to the Shushan Palace by tomorrow morn."

The town buzzed with excitement. Many people wondered about the strange decree; nothing like this had ever happened. "What was going on?" Women ran home, covering their young daughters' faces with wraps. "Why?" asked a stranger in a brown tunic, "that is a strange request even from a King!" Others joined in the protest. "Yes, why must our young maidens report to the palace?"

The people did not like King Dawit. He was harsh and unkind, oppressing them with high agriculture, manufacturing, and temple taxes. The Persians and

Medes were not required to pay taxes, and this unfair practice and injustice angered them.

"What's going on in the royal palace?" asked an old lady pulling a stubborn goat. "The King continues to offend us. Now this new decree, for our young maidens. Is there any justice in the land for the common people!" cried the stranger in the brown tunic.

Several skirmishes broke out in the plaza as the people started throwing stones and rocks at the royal soldiers. The inhabitants did not know what was happening. Some suspected the Queen had been beheaded like a commoner. Others thought the King had gone insane; he was known for strange behavior, but a few knew he was rebuilding the royal harem. Queen Zenia had dishonored him, and he had secretly put her away.

Amara, a 15-year-old orphan, lived in Susa with her Uncle Kaleb and Aunt Martha. They were exiles from Jerusalem, yet Kaleb served faithfully in the King's Court. He kept his ethnicity to himself and cautioned the women to do the same thing. Amara's parents had both been murdered during one of the many wars. "Pack your belongings, Amara. I must take you to the King's palace! Amara, Amara!" Kaleb called excitedly.

"The palace," said Martha, "why do you have to take Amara to the palace?"

"The King's decree, he wants all the virgin lovelies there by morn," said Uncle Kaleb. "If we leave now, we will make it on time."

"Why, Kaleb?" asked his wife, concerned.

"I do not know why, but we are foreigners from another land, and I do not want any problems with the officials. Remember whom I work for."

"Uncle Kaleb, could it be that the decree is only for the Persian citizens?" asked Amara.

"The decree was not clear, but one thing is clear," said Kaleb. "The King wants the virgin lovelies in the providence. Amara, you fit that portrait. It could be a census he is taking. You must hurry and pack just a few things. It will only be a few days."

The young girl reluctantly started walking toward her chambers. She wanted to avoid going to the King's palace. There were rumors Queen Zenia had grown a tail for disobeying the Shah and was tormenting young girls. *Was that even possible?* Amara wondered.

"Kaleb, I do not think the palace is a good place for Amara," whispered Martha. "I hear the Queen has grown a tail for disobeying the King."

"She refused to appear naked before him and his officials and was banished from the King's presence." Kaleb laughed, "Where is your mind? Is it that she had grown a tail?" *How foolish*, he thought.

"That's even more concerning," Martha said, appalled. "I do not blame her for refusing. If Zenia had appeared before the guest disrobed when the King himself was lightheaded with wine, she would have been seen as a mere concubine. By God, she did the correct thing and should not be punished. I would have done the same." Kaleb looked dubiously at his wife. Could Queen Zenia's refusal to obey her husband have already begun to infect the other women in the providence, including his wife?

"Amara is a lovely maiden, and in time, the King will look at her beauty," Martha continued, "I am worried for her."

"The head eunuch will stand guard over the virgins, and the royal army will protect them as well," said Kaleb. "And I will protect her," he assured Martha.

Secretly, Kaleb hoped Amara would become Queen so that he could be promoted to Vizier, a high-ranking political advisor to the King. Zenia had been a thorn in the flesh of Mother Queen Adi since she arrived at the palace. Besides, Zenia almost got him killed by her tiger.

He did not like her; she was aggressive and dared to slap him with her slipper when he went to get her at the King's request.

Kaleb was one of the men who had taunted the King to show the Queen naked as a trophy. This would teach her to be arrogant and prideful. He remembered that night. The King was vulnerable, lightheaded, and drunk on wine. The heckling and mocking by his leaders made him feel ignominious. He finally agreed to show her, but only for a short time.

The leaders were merry, drinking and taking bets among themselves. "Will the Queen join us? I bet ten shekels of silver she will not appear," called out Kaleb. "I bet two gold shekels she will appear!" cried a general. The men laughed and taunted the King while placing their bets, saying, "Diversity in counsel, unity in command… the Queen leads the battle, for there is no man!" King Dawit was highly offended when Queen Zenia refused his request, for he had wagered and lost a large estate to one of the generals.

Martha interrupted Kaleb's thoughts, "Many women that have gone to the harem have been killed, mutilated, and burned alive. Who protected them?"

"Hush, woman! You know the penalty for speaking against the royal crown," Kaleb whispered.

"I speak not against the royal crown," she whispered back, "It is not safe for Amara to be in the harem. My brother would have died first before putting his daughter in a harem! Are you forgetting how much she has been through already?" Martha cried, her voice trembling. "We can pretend Amara is underage. She looks young enough."

"That could get us both killed, woman. Lying to the King is a capital offense!"

"Why do I have to go?" Amara asked, entering the dining area with a few of her items.

"It's the King's decree, sealed with his signet ring, that all young virgins report to the palace by morn. I don't know what it's all about. It could be a census for taxation, he lied, "but you will not be the only maiden there."

"Uncle Kaleb, will I become one of the King's concubines?" Amara asked, her large blue eyes tearing up. She thought of Todd, the young Satrap, and the Governor of Susa. They had been secretly meeting for some time to share their affection.

"No, my little blue Jay," Kaleb said, embracing her. "You are not going to become one of the King's concubines; you might become the queen," he humored her. "The King might not even notice you, and you can return to us within a week."

"What if he notices me? Will he brand me like an animal and keep me in a herd of women? I should have died with my parents!" cried Amara, crushed in spirit. She thought of running to Todd for advice, but time did not allow it.

Martha embraced Amara; her heart was heavy with grief, for deep inside, she knew it would be the last time she would probably see her. They wept bitterly. Going to the King's palace was never good for a young virgin. The ones that did come back would be defiled in mind and body, their innocence taken from them. Many would become temple prostitutes, while others became beggars in the street. No righteous man would have a defiled maiden. The family may find a suitor if the young girl is stunning, but the bride's value would be diminished. Amara was a humble, modest, elegant girl, and the debaucherous lifestyle in the palace was genuinely concerning.

In front of the Shushan Palace, a long line of virgins started to form as far as the eye could see. Zenia stood on the balcony watching as the line continued to grow, even in the rain. One of these damsels would soon replace her, the future was uncertain.

CHAPTER THREE

THE WARNING

The howling winds outside had woken King Dawit from another disturbing dream. He reached for Queen Zenia to be comforted and help interpret his dreams, but she was not next to him. Unable to sleep, he stepped out on the balcony to gaze at the sky. The starless sky was a blanket of thick, gritty haze and ominous orange clouds. *Another storm on the horizon?* He thought about the dream, what did it mean?

"Dawit, the Great King of the Achaemenid Empire," he mocked himself. "The best men are made from many faults, but in the end, neither greatness nor fame will deliver from the hand of judgment." His countenance was downcast, with invisible heavy shackles.

The son and successor of King Darius the Great, Dawit was a giant of a man in stature but lacked discernment.

He could not read the intentions of the human heart and was easily beguiled and misled, especially by his mother. The diverse prophets in the royal court rarely predicted or interpreted his dreams correctly. No one dared to speak omens over the King; Mother Queen Adi would have them beheaded. The King was incomprehensibly wealthy, cruel, and a womanizer, but who dared to hold him accountable?

People in Susa greatly feared the King, but they adored Queen Zenia. The women, especially, beheld the Queen, for she was kind, always giving alms to the poor, gifting them with Persian textile, grains, incense, and even gold bracelets. During plagues, she would send the royal healers to treat their infirmities. The common people were not the only ones who loved Zenia.

The King summoned his advisors to the palace. They arrived one by one and took their counsel seats. Many were concerned the King had recollections of what happened at the banquet. They were pleasantly surprised to hear why the King had called a council meeting.

"I had a dream that made me concerned." A cacophony of comments stirred the room. They talked among themselves, being careful not to offend the King.

"Tell us about the dream," said Artabanus, faking concern. He was the brother of Mother Queen and the father of Todd.

King Dawit waited until all the chattering quieted, for he wanted their full attention. "A large griffin appeared as I was lying in bed, and I rode on its back as I would ride a horse. We flew over a large ocean body of endless islands. Suddenly, a woman's hand ascended beneath the sea, ensnaring the griffin."

The advisors sat in silence for a long time. They did not know what to think about the dream, but others knew it was an omen, a warning, or the handwriting on the wall.

"I commend the wise men of the Achaemenid Empire to come and interpret the dream," King Dawit said, breaking the silence. The magicians, enchanters, astrologers, and diviners were all sanctioned to the courts. Many tingled the ears of the King with falsehood and faltering, but none dared to speak of gloom and doom.

Finally, one of the Magi came into the presence of the King. He was rarely called upon, for he only interpreted the reading before him, which was not always good. The Magi was a serious man with cold, dark eyes. He carried a clay model of a sheep's liver he had sacrificed for the reading.

The leaders waited as the Magi referenced a scroll with numbers and symbols only, he could understand.

"For the King of the Achaemenid Empire standeth at the parting of the way, at the head of the two ways. A voyage is at hand with the cries of battles. Storms rage from the deep sea. A warning, the water nymph, daughter of Nereus, lures boatmen into destruction."

The reading infuriated some generals, who faulted the Magi for having had too much haoma. "Perhaps the Magi is absent-minded with too much drink," said one of the generals. Other leaders disagreed with the oracles of the Magi. Artabanus, the primary instigator, spoke first. "Delay not the campaign to the Aegean Islands," he cried. "Eight years have been spent preparing for the campaign. Indeed, the Greeks make a mockery of us. We must not delay and must continue the work thy father began!"

"Fear ye not that the dream speaks of destruction; nevertheless, let's consult with the celestials and confirm the oracle of the Magi," said Gabe. He believed the oracles and the dream warned the King, but he needed more confirmation.

"Swiftly, we should move to put down the uprisings of the Aegean; they are inhabiting an inheritance that must be claimed," said another general. "Remember, our army is better equipped than their despairing population, a country separated in conflict. Delay not while their forces strengthen."

"Remember, ill omens kill Kings and ruin countries," warned the Magi. "King Dawit has offended Ahura Mazda by following the lie. Yet the King wants the mighty hand to extend into foreign lands to campaign. He pledges alliance with others, but his land is ravished with taxes and disarrays. His attempts to subjugate the Aegean will not go well for Your Majesty."

"Dare you speak to the King in that tone," said Gabe, taking out his whip.

"Do not flog the Magi," intervened King Dawit. "Thy oracles are well spoken, for I have followed the lie. Go and give sacrifice offerings to Ahura Mazda so I might find favor in his sight and be strengthened for the Spring campaign."

The King was thought to be gullible and inexperienced, listening to the Magi; others thought it was wise to appease

Ahura Mazda, especially before a campaign. "We will offer gold and silver to keep the holy fire burning day and night," said Artabanus.

King Dawit followed the ways of Ahura Mazda, the one and true God. Unlike the Hebrew God, who formed men out of dust, Ahura Mazda created men out of fire. His teaching taught the world was an endless battlefield between good and evil.

Ahura Mazda was the all-wise bounteous, undeceiving creator of everything good. The thoughts, words, and actions of the King were to reflect the attributes of Ahura Mazda for him to ascend into paradise in the afterlife. The late Prophet Zoroaster described the coexistence of forces of good and evil in the spiritual realm, the free will to choose; King Dawit knew this, but he did not always make the right choices.

The Magi faced the Sun; he swayed back and forth and dropped to his knees, singing a hymn:

"I shall raise an altar unto thy divine. The fire burning in thy hearts as a sanctuary. My Atharvan will ye be, and I tend the holy fire within. I exhort thee to cleanse thy body and bring fuel to the fire that may burn bright, dutifully, and purify thy mind and the cleanliness of thy heart. As the sacred fire flickers on the altar of thy heart and kindle into a blazing flame heavenward, may ye rise upward unto thee."

CHAPTER FOUR

THE ADVISORS

Gabe was a 35-year-old burly Medes with bright red curly hair and a round beard that extended to his chest. He was the chief advisor and royal bodyguard of the King. His living quarters were next to the Shah's, and his sleep had been disturbed when he heard King Dawit speaking out loud.

There had been several attempts on King Dawit's life since he usurped the crown. King Dawit was an infamous king who lived by the sword, slaughtering those who conspired against him and was a blatant womanizer. Gabe had his own opinions on how the King was draining the empire's coffers with his elaborate parties, immense palaces, building projects, and now a beauty competition to select a new Queen.

These thoughts, secretly concealed in Gabe's heart, did not change his obligations toward the King. He knew there was no reason to lose his head for his opinions. Gabe wondered if the King had gone mad when he removed Queen Zenia from the throne. The King had been acting peculiarly, he noticed.

"His Majesty-exalted Shah!" Gabe rushed into the King's chambers with a dagger in his left hand. He was determined to defend the King, as was his duty. "His Majesty is all well with thee?"

"It was a nightmare which disturbed my sleep," King Dawit answered, his countenance low.

"Shall I summon the astrologers to help you interpret the dream?" Gabe asked, scanning the room cautiously. Ambushes were common and occasionally plotted by the Shah himself.

"Have a seat," King Dawit said, motioning to a chair. The room was still dimly illuminated with the flickering of oil lamps, casting large shadows on the wall. Gabe sat by the exit door with his eyes facing the balcony. Outside, the sun had not risen, and there was frost on the ground. He heard crackling ice and saw a shadow on a steed galloping toward the south gate. Who could be traveling so early? he wondered.

"Hold not thy truth from me," said the King, his eyes burning with fire. "Who dared to mock me at the banquet? I will feed them to the lions."

Gabe did not like it when the King was downcast, for he did evil things. "There were many," Gabe said. King Dawit's eyes were wild with fear. "Many? I am afraid my behavior offended Ahura Mazda," he said, looking at the giant figure behind his bed. The King appeared to be feeling guilty.

"Who advised the decree to banish the Queen?" The King asked. Gabe remembered it was the eunuch who suggested it, and Mother Queen had sealed the decree with the King's signet ring. "It was you," Gabe said. He knew better than to tell the truth, as he did not want his head to end on the chopping block. The King had been drunk on wine and would not remember.

"I recollect not much of what occurred," the King admitted. Gabe's left eye twitched. He was the King's bodyguard and would defend him to the death. But he did not like to be put in a quagmire of confusion. It was not his idea to banish the Queen. He had nothing but respect and admiration for her.

"Do you not remember? You became outraged! When the Queen disobeyed your orders to present herself to the guest in only her crown." King Dawit scratched the back of his ears and sat on his bed. "What more did I do or say," the King encouraged.

"I do not know why you made a strange request," said Gabe.

Gabe hesitated and wondered if it was advantageous to tell the King everything. The King's advisors had wanted to order the Queen's execution. Gabe stopped their relentless taunting, warning them of an insurrection from the people if something happened to Zenia. That would have been a bad omen.

"I cannot believe I was so foolish," Dawit confessed. Gabe nodded in silence. He agreed the King had been foolish and lacked wisdom but held his peace.

King Dawit recollects the day his father brought two young damsels to the Susa Palace. The one with the dirty face was far from a helpless, docile maiden. He was a young prince who had traveled to distant places, done many things, and seen many women but had never seen a more beautiful creature.

His father handed both girls to Haggai, the eunuch. "Father, "Who are they?"

"These are spoils from the war, my son."

"Spoils, what do you mean spoils? They are princesses from Babylon. I was the stable boy of their father."

His father laughed, "They are princesses; I found them in the Palace of King Belshazzar. The dirty-faced one is a tigress; be careful with her; she bites."

Shortly after, Dawit deployed to Greece. One day, Prince Dawit was at the palace, standing on the marble balcony, admiring the vastness of his kingdom, when a maiden came from behind and tapped him on the shoulders, "Got you," she said. "Now, you must chase me." She laughed as she ran away playfully. The girl ran like a Gazelle, leaping over statutes, structures, and stones. It was hard to keep up with her as she jumped, rolled, and twirled further away from him. He was still recovering from a minor battle injury but refused to give up the pursuit, determined to catch his prey. Seeing that he lingered behind, she slowed down, and he caught her and took her into his arms. She was perspiring and breathless, but her long tresses smelled like lavender.

"I seized you and have claim over the territory," he said, breathless. His eyes fastened, and his heart smote, yearning after Zenia.

"I guess you did," she answered in a low voice, tickling him until he let her go, and she ran from him.

In Dawit's absence, Zenia had grown into a beautiful woman; a tigress, untamed, unspoiled, unpossessed, and unnatural for such a beautiful being… and his father loved her.

Zenia was spoiled and treated as an Empress, which infuriated Mother Queen. She had King Darius wrapped around her finger and entered the throne room without waiting for the scepter to be extended. The young maiden possessed many notable qualities: intelligence, savvy, and loved playing the King's game. His father had lost several estates to her clever game strategies. One day, it was King Darius' birthday. It was customary on the King's birthday to give a wish to the family members. At the time, he was the crowned prince and asked for Zenia, surprising both his parents. 'Splendid choice,' replied King Darius, and the marriage was immediately arranged. Mother Queen was devastated and retaliated by giving Zenia's sister in marriage to the leader of Caria.

A knock on the door interrupted the King's thoughts. Who would be calling so early in the morning? He wondered. His advisors filed in one by one—men of courage, strength, and pride. The leaders, generals, and satraps came to discuss battle strategies and travel plans. As the chiefs gathered, King Dawit watched.

He was still saddle-sore from losing the Battle of Marathon and looking for vengeance. "The battle was my father's attempt to punish Athens and Eretria for interfering with his plans," said King Dawit resentfully. The generals listened attentively. Many of them had fought in that battle.

"All was going well for the Persian campaign," agreed Gabe. "First, the island of Naxos was razed with fire. Then, we island-hopped to the Cycladic Islands and brought them under the Persian Empire." The leaders all gestured in agreement; they did have the upper hand.

"Eretria was besieged and razed before we headed toward Attica, landing on Marathon on the way to Athens," King Dawit said, fuming.

"That's when we came face to face with a smaller Athenian army. Their soldiers were formidable, with military training. They start training their boys at age seven, making them brutal for battle," Todd chimed in.

"King Darius' health started failing, and he died before completing his quest," said Gabe, his voice grieved.

"I will punish Athens for interfering with my father's plan. This time, it would be different; I would lead the massive military myself, punish them, and extend the Achaemenid Empire into the western frontier. I will complete what my father has started."

The Greeks had made a mockery of the undefeatable Persian army, and Dawit was looking for Greek skin to fashion into a throne. "I swear I will bring those Hellenes to subjugation. The sword shall slay them," said the King.

Gabe remembered them to be strong, intelligent, and strong in battle. He was a mighty warrior and lost his right hand in the war. He knew the strength of a man is tested in battle, and the Greeks had been tested victoriously.

"Here I make an end of my anger," said the King to the men, "and let us put the past behind us to make haste. Is the channel across the peninsula of Mount completed? "What about the bridge of Mt. Athos?" Gabe was relieved that the King had a change of thoughts and started to focus on battle plans. There was still much to be completed before the Spring.

CHAPTER FIVE

THE CITY OF SUSA

The Achaemenid Empire was an expansive estate stretching from the deserts of Libya in the West to the Indus River Valley in the east, toward Central Asia in the North, and to the Nile in the south. The colossal land was divided into twenty provinces and appointed satrapies. They were governed by princes of the Persian royal family established by King Dawit, who gave them power and authority, dispensing justice, collecting tributes, and providing security on the empire's borders. The Persians were given special privileges and hired as top government officials.

Their cousins, the Medes, were the military elites, the Immortals, the Garrisons, and the Mercenaries of the royal army. The citizens lived a free lifestyle, running their businesses by buying, selling, or contracting with the government. Special consideration as scribes and translators was given to anyone who spoke, read, or wrote in one of the three main languages: Avesta, Parthian, or Bactrian.

There were four significant cities: Parsagadae, Persepolis, Susa, and Ecbatana. Susa was the seat of the government, where the imperial court resided. Ecbatana was Media's capital and the Achaemenian King's summer retreat. Pasargadae was a large metropolis of diverse culture, rich in art, architecture, monuments, and gardens, a city established by the late King Cyrus. Persepolis was the ceremonial capital of the Achaemenid Empire, well hidden in the walled plains of Marvdasht, southern Zagros mountains. This city was safe, and nobles and tributaries were invited to celebrate the Nowruz holiday, the Persian New Year, a festive celebration during the Spring Equinox. It was the best-kept secret where the King stored rare and royal gifts presented or confiscated from conquered lands.

Life with Aunt Martha and Uncle Kaleb was good for Amara. Uncle Kaleb was in the King's inner circle.

Poverty never worried her. Her uncle earned enough gold to keep the family well-provided with plenty of house servants to help with the estate's daily chores and administration. Amara was a good girl accepting domesticity as a daughter, a humble Hebrew girl, not seeking public recognition. She tightened her cloak under her chin and pulled her hood to keep the rain off her face. She was grim and gloomy as they journeyed, two ghosts in the rainstorm. The donkey splashed water along the puddled muddy road. "Abba, why must I report to the Shushan Palace?" she asked again.

"I told you, Amara, it is the King's decree."

"I don't understand what it means."

Kaleb took a deep breath; he was getting agitated with the continued questioning. He was only looking out for Amara. The young girl did not understand what it would mean if she became the next Queen of Persia, a life of royalty all the days of her life.

He tried to explain it again.

"The mulish queen has been removed from the throne for disobeying the King. That happens when women are disobedient," he said, cautioning. "A new queen will replace that rebellious woman."

"What has that to do with me? I come not from royal blood," she said. Amara did not know she was a descendant of the infamous King Saul, the first Monarch of Israel.

"For that reason, you have nothing to fear; we just obey the King's decree," Kaleb asserted.

The palace was closer than Amara thought. They had traveled in the gusting winds of driving rain, and she was fatigued. Riding on a donkey was a challenging ride to Susa, sixty-two miles from the mouth of the Tigris. It stood on plains from Babylonian alluvium. The southwest connected Susa to Babylon, surrounded by mountains. To the West was the long, narrow ridge of the Kabir Kuh. Directly North were the southeast ranges of Zagros, and southeast of them was the higher central mountain mass. Amara could see gravelly conglomerate hills and reddish sandstone marking the drop of the alluvium.

Summers in Susa were intolerable. The surrounding mountains intercepted cooling northerly winds, and even lizards and snakes burned to death in the noon heat. Icy water exposed to the Sun immediately heated baths, and barley spread out to dry, pop-like grain parched in an oven. November weather began to cool the plains as the winds turned northeast, and wheat and barley were in season. By mid-month, the rains and winds veered to the southeast and east. Hailstorms were frequent. Snow flurries reached the plain in Winter, and temperatures dropped below freezing.

Traveling in the opposite direction was Queen Zenia. She felt optimistic for the first time in days. The south wind stung her ears. Frost crunched under her horse's hooves as she galloped out of the south gate. Zenia dressed in a black hooded leather tunic over a colt skin dress and knee-high squirrel skin boots. The gate guard was nowhere in sight, and this was her opportunity to leave without being noticed.

A chilly wind whipped across Amara's freezing face. The sound of mournful jackals filled the air, sending shivers up her spine. "We are almost there." Uncle Kaleb announced. Suddenly, he saw a person on horseback approaching and passing them in the opposite direction.

Zenia could see a hunched-shouldered man pulling a young maiden on a donkey. She covered her face and quickly drove past them. The man looked familiar, but not the young damsel. Kaleb flashed a glance as the horse trotted past them but could not see who it was. The horse stomped and splashed mud over him. It had to be one of the King's messengers on a mission. Who else would be out in this weather?

They passed the outskirts of Shush toward the Shushan Palace. Amara could not help noticing the erected monumental landscapes on temple platforms with beautiful and handmade ceramic pots designed on limestones with images of goats' heads with fish tails. Offerings to their deity, she thought.

More commanding than a pyramid, a massive ziggurat stood in the city's center, enclosed with numerous temples. Around the town were two canals joined by a network of bank mounds connected by colored-bricked buildings and houses of lime mixed with sand. It looked like the Processional Road to the Ishtar Gate in Sippar.

The city opened up, crammed with people. Young maidens and their escorts jammed together shoulder to shoulder, jostling for space like spectators. It was also deafening. The rain did little to deaden the clamor. Raising her voice above the noise, Amara asked, "Are these maidens here for the decree?" Kaleb smiled. "That's correct, there is much competition."

They passed the town, buzzing with excitement. The street widened as they approached the entrance of the palace. This was the center of the intellectual, religious, and cultural powers and the political center of the King and his Winter home. The display, in its splendor, took Amara's breath away. It was incredible.

The sand was topped with foundations of well-made bricks, which supported halls of pillars, with porticoes to sides and front, guarded by square towers. The apadana ground was layered with pebbles and lime mortar washed with red coloring. Limestone columns of double volute with figures of animals, floral designs, ionic capitals, and members of the Ten Thousand Immortals dressed in rich dresses covered the walls.

At the center of the eastern wall of the palace, there was a three-thousand-foot gateway with solid towers at both sides. Finely baked bricks on the walls of these towers formed relief figures of stalking and seated lions, winged bulls and griffins with goats' horns, lions' forepaws and tails, and eagles' claws instead of hind paws. There was also a heraldic of the lion killing the golden-hoofed white bull that caught Amara's eye. "Abba, what is the meaning of that heraldic?" She asked, pointing at the lion killing the golden-hoofed bull.

"That represents the defeat of Winter, the bull, by the Spring Equinox, the lion. The celebration of Nowruz; it's like Rosh Hashanah is to us."

"Is it a sacred day?" Amara asked curiously.

"For the Persian people, yes. They celebrate the first day of Spring, the 21st day of March, feasting with family and friends and exchanging gifts. The children play with colorful eggs." Uncle Kaleb smiled, showing his uneven teeth.

"The exact date of Rosh Hashanah varies yearly, based on our Hebrew Calendar. Our rites celebrate the world's birthday with shofar blowing and penitence for ten days. During this ten-day, the God of Israel judges all creatures and, on Yom Kippur, decides who will live or die in the coming year. The names of the righteous are written in the Book of Life, and the wicked are condemned."

Amara did not particularly like celebrating Rosh Hashanah. It was a gloomy time for her. The memories of her parents' murder on New Year's left her empty. When she heard the shofar blow during the tekiah, she always cried. No one knew the anguish of her suffering.

"King Darius built this palace." Uncle Kaleb said, trying to lighten up the heavy load on Amara. Suddenly, she looked despondent, and he wanted to change the mood. The maiden had been gloomy since they left town, and he did not want her to feel sad.

"King Darius," she repeated absentmindedly. Amara stood for a moment, taking it in. Life will never be the same. She suddenly felt the urge to cry.

The crying pierced the quiet of the morning as Zenia listened intensely. The sounds came from a nearby den.

CHAPTER SIX

GIRLS, GIRLS, GIRLS

"Quick, get some warm wet linens, Rosie!" ordered Mother Queen Adi. Rosie hurried around the woman's house as fast as her short legs could carry her. Hordes of virgins arrived from the entire empire. The most beautiful virgins in the Persian Dynasty arrive on horseback, camels, elephants, caravans, and some even donkeys. The torrent weather did not foreshorten their travel. The maidens had never been to the Shushan Palace.

The palace was separate from the city. One had to cross over a river, walk through the King's Gate, and into three large courtyards. The King's throne was in a great hall on the grand walkway through the palace.

No one was allowed to enter the courtroom without the King extending his scepter. The penalty for doing so was death. The women's houses were through the palace's middle courtyard and into the inner court. Rosie recruited several servants to assist with the maidens. The castle was full of virgins eagerly waiting in line.

Rosie was from Elam, the Highlands East of Babylon. The Assyrians had subjugated her country, ravaging the land with fire and swords. Her mother was one of the few who had survived the slaughter and was exiled to Susa as a servant to the King. She was a wise woman, devoted to the care of the Royal family, winning their trust. After her mother's death, Rosie succeeded her as the head of the Royal Housekeepers. In all fairness, Rosie was pleasant, with large brown eyes and a warm smile. She never knew who her father was, but many servants in the palace did not know their fathers. Her mother never talked about it.

Amara followed the crowd toward the palace. Uncle Kaleb escorted her but redirected her from the crowd when they reached the palace's entrance. "Abba, look, there is where the women wait," she said, pointing at the girls lining up. Her brows knitted angrily, trying to understand why her uncle chose to stay in Susa working with a ruthless King. She wished she had died with her parents.

"I know a different way to the head eunuch. He awaits in the women's harem." Kaleb was not allowed in the women's court. Amara followed him; her nerves wound taut; somehow, something was amidst. She could feel it in her gut but could not pinpoint it.

It was not the head eunuch waiting in the women's court when they entered; it was Adi. Kaleb was startled. The older woman was perched on a chair like a crow on a tree stump. He stumbled over his words. "O' Queen, you will live forever," he blurted out.

Mother Queen held up her hand to stop him. Kaleb fidgeted, too tense to swallow. Amara studied his face, trying to read his intentions, for he had plans, and Amara could not guess what they were.

"Dare you enter the women's chamber," said Mother Queen. Kaleb stood in silence, his heart racing inside his chest. He had to think fast. "The eunuch is not here?" he asked. "My niece. It's her first time away from home, and she is very anxious. I hoped Haggai could help quiet her spirit," he said in a whimpering voice; obviously lying.

Mother Queen looked at the scared young woman, who was playing along with the story like a puppet on a string. "Leave her with me," she said sharply, ushering Amara behind a closed door. Kaleb was left outside, wondering if he had set poor Amara in a dreadful situation.

Dawit was Mother Queen's favorite son, and she knew how to humor him, exerting much influence on him. It was her idea to be placed in charge of the virgins. She would watch over them as a shepherdess watches over the flocks. The girls will be appropriately trained to be pleasing to the King, not rebellious, like Queen Zenia. She would evaluate the girls before presenting them to her son and ensure he was never embarrassed again.

"Thy help is not necessary," Queen Mother announced to the self-appointed panel of men as she entered the hall; Amara nervously followed. Rosie appeared with servants, hot, scented water, basins, and linens.

Girls from every province in the Achaemenid Empire. It was something new to the excited, joyful, and eager young women: a beauty contest. There was an exuberant, ebullience release of energy that Rosie had never felt in the palace before. The air was full of free-flowing laughter, chatter, and the giggles of maidens. Some were tall, short, pretty, not-so-pretty, elegant, plain, and bouncy, but most importantly, they were virgins.

Raising her hand, Mother Queen entered the hall. The room suddenly went quiet. They all knew she was the one and only Mother Queen. The women prostrated before the majestic goddess, who stood in her elegance and grace, much older but impressive. Amara bowed with the other girls. They had no idea what they were signing up for, but the novelty of becoming like Mother Queen was a dream come true, an opportunity of a lifetime.

The head eunuch, Haggai, entered the hall shortly and stood by Mother Queen. Top officials have bombarded him all morning regarding their daughters, offering gifts of silver and gold for the twelve-moon purification period. Many were the daughters of the royal extended family, the highest of the land.

"My servant Rosie will prepare you for the andaruni after the feet washing," announced Queen Mother in her caregiving voice. She was excessive with cleansing.

"Does that mean the women's house?" whispered Vanessa, a dark-complexioned beautiful girl from Ethiopia.

"I know not," Amara said, staring straight ahead to avoid meeting anybody's eyes. She had to force herself to hold her head high. How can her uncle do this to her? They were a Hebrew family and should have returned to Zion to help build the temple of God. The thought infuriated her. She just wanted to run away and hide.

Rosie washed Amara's feet and wiped them dry with linen; shortly after, Haggai, the head eunuch, approached Amara. They were not strangers; he remembered her as a little girl. She had a solemn face, a high nose, and long, thick locks. The damsel was meek and obedient, easygoing, peaceful, and friendly. All the children liked it when she organized the activities because all were included. Look at her now, he thought, a ravaging, beautiful young woman. Her Uncle Kaleb spoke highly of her, and she was a highborn descendant of King Saul.

Amara wondered how everything had gone wrong. Her uncle had a fortune, so he only subjected her to this humiliation for himself, for he was an ambitious man, leading her like a sheep to the slaughter.

Zenia was on the road least traveled. The late King Cyrus thought he was smart after building the Royal Road, but the Persians were no wiser. Their ideas came from the subjugated states. Alphabets, strategies, and innovations were integrated to enhance their empire. The Royal Road was one of many ways to Babylon. Years before the Persians were even a people, the Babylonians built roads, secret routes, and underground tunnels to transfer material to make ziggurats. The Tower of Babel, the road to heaven, was one of the projects they worked on when the construction stopped suddenly. Years later, Zenia's grandfather Nebuchadnezzar funded a project hoping to recover the lost blueprints. As a child, she heard stories of how God, from heaven, had stopped the construction and scattered the people to the four corners of the world.

It was a nine-day trip on horseback from Susa to Babylon on the Royal Road, but that's not why Zenia avoided it. It was also the most traveled road, facilitating communication from the King to his distant subjects. There was a shorter cut, a stringent, rigorous path, but the trip would only take eighteen hours.

Wild animals of all kinds lived in the deserted part of the Zagros mountains: Persian Leopards, Brown Bears, and Asiatic Lions, but the sudden vociferous, piercing sound Zenia heard was not the cry of an animal. The rains had stopped, and the winds had died down. Zenia's heart was racing inside her chest as she followed the cries. It was coming from inside a den. Frightened but compelled, she stepped onto the frozen ground and dismounted the horse, her bow and poison arrows on her shoulders. Her stomach was watery with nerves. It was still dark and cold. The sounds did not sound like the cries of a wild animal. This was an unfamiliar cry, like a whiny, nasal, continuous cry that intensified with urgency. Zenia stood at the gape of the dark den, contemplating.

She could see there was an obscure figure on the cold ground. From what she could see, it was not a four-legged animal. The piercing cries came from that direction. Cautiously, she entered the den. As her eyes adjusted to the darkness, she realized it was a woman on the ground who looked injured. The cries came from something between the woman's legs wiggling on the floor. Zenia jumped back; what was it?

She drew a little closer...was it what she thought?

It was a human babe in a pool of blood.

Zenia approached the woman on the ground, shaking her. "Ye look hurt," said Zenia, but the girl was unresponsive. Her eyes were opened but void of life. The damsel was dead, but her body was still warm. *She must have just died,* thought Zenia. The crying, wrinkled baby was still attached, swimming in a large puddle of blood. Queen Zenia had to do something, or the baby would die. She thought the umbilical cord must be cut, reaching for the dagger she carried strapped on her thigh. Quickly, she removed a gold hairpin from her hair and twisted it into a clasp. Using her dagger, she severed the umbilical cord and bound it with the hair clip. The wiggling babe was slimy in blood, his eyes closed shut and angry. It was a male child. She swaddled the baby using the mother's scarf to keep it warm.

Queen Zenia was in awe at the squirming crying baby. He was trying to eat his little hand and must be hungry. She looked for provisions, but there was nothing. *What was the mother doing out here by herself during childbirth? Was she a slave girl who ran from her taskmaster?*

The mother was not a shepherdess; they would not be in the high mountains that time of year. The maiden was about Zenia's age. Her clothing would suggest she was not from the local area. Perhaps she was a goddess, Zenia humored herself. It did not matter. The crying baby needed nutrients. It would be hours before she reached her destination, and the child may not survive the long journey without nourishment. The wailing child made Zenia feel desperate. She looked around the den for something to feed him. The body of the mother was still warm. She wondered if the mother had milk. When she found Amber, her tiger, she nursed the cub with the mother's milk; although she was dead, maybe it would work.

She took the baby and laid it on the mother's breast. Immediately, he started suckling. How did he know to do that?

The Sun was rising when Zenia was ready to continue her journey. She had wrapped the child in a blanket she fashioned from the mother's wrap and strapped the baby on her back. Exiting the den, she saw a lion about a hundred yards away. Her heart dropped to her feet. It was a large, buffish grey color lion with amber eyes and a scanty mane on both cheeks and throat.

An omen, a vision, or a test? she thought.

Frozen with fear, she stood, not wanting to draw attention. If the lion walks away, it is foretelling, but if the lion charges her, it's not a vision but a test.

It seemed like hours, but it was only a few seconds; Zenia had to think swiftly. The proud, mature lion was not retreating; was the den its pride area? She did not want to kill it. As long as she kept her distance, her chances of survival were reasonably good. Sometimes, one must kill or be killed, and she feared the outcome. Animals were special to her, and she would not harm them unless her life was in danger. The lion watched from its distance. Go away, she thought, wondering if animals could read her thoughts. Gracefully, she pulled out an arrow. Spare thyself, and spare me, I mourn thy death. The lion continued to stare sternly and majestically. The horse was getting edgy, and so was Zenia. She aimed and could make a clear shot but wished he would leave. Astonishingly, the lion turned around and slowly walked away in the opposite direction. Zenia breathed a sigh of relief and thanked God the babe had not woken up. Mounting the horse, she continued on her journey. It was not until she was more relaxed that she thought about the baby.

CHAPTER SEVEN

THE MIGHTY GREEKS

I n the twinkle of an eye, a widespread eclipse caused a significant collapse in the Eastern Mediterranean world, shattering the motherland of Greece. The sea and the earth swallowed everything, and for four hundred years, the land was desolate. From these fragments rose the Greeks, an amphibious being. Mariners were driven toward the Aegean islands, not because of the sirens' songs but because of the mysterious shadow hills that rose to the heavens like temples. Two thousand islands were scattered as far as an eye could see on the Mediterranean Sea. One could leap from one island to another.

These islands were situated in southern Europe. Each island had its own culture and customs but shared a common language. Forming a central government was brutal, and there was contention and discord between the dwellers of the islands. It was a time of advancements for the Greek people, with new frontiers and expansions.

On the other side of the Mediterranean Sea was another group of dwellers, the Persians. They were a collected clan of enterprising people under the rulership of one King. The Persian Dynasty was an undefeatable, advancing, growing, forceful regime.

The men from Persia were tall, rough, hardy, solid, hairy men with piercing eyes and striking, robust features. They wrapped their thick hair in turbans to endure the desert's heat, dust, and dry climate. The merchants traveled on dromedaries in the blistering heat to distant lands to sell their commodities of wheat, oats, rice, barley, figs, sheep, goats, and crafts. These vendors traveled in caravans from city to city, sharing information as they advanced their goods.

In comparison, the Greek men were ivory athletes, handsome, strong, intelligent men who wore weaved wreaths and long togas. They spend much time in public meetings debating frivolous arguments, leading to contention and strife among them. They spent hours exercising, anointing their naked bodies in gymnasiums, for the Olympic competitions. It was their religious practice in honor of Zeus, the God of the sky. Zeus was the ruler, protector, and father of all gods and humans. Each city-state had its local deity. As a people, they did not agree on anything, and they loved fighting.

The Grecian lands took a lot of work to cultivate. Most people made their living on farming, growing olive trees, fishing, and trading.

Others were soldiers, scholars, scientists, and artists. The cities had beautiful temples, stone columns, statues, and open-air theaters. Some lived from piracy, exploiting sea merchants who traveled on the Mediterranean Sea from Western Asia, North Africa, and Southern Europe.

Over the years, the Persians and the Greeks collided. The Greek city-states had fought hard and furious to earn their independence successfully. The Persians' territories stretched from Northern India to Southeast Europe and had already subjugated wealthy Greek Ionian colonies in Western Anatolia. Their army was unstoppable. King Dawit aspired to complete his father's mission expanding across the Mediterranean Sea to the remaining Aegean Islands.

Even though Greek city-states had differences, they had one thing in common: Democracy. They would not allow the beast of the Southwest to devour them one island at a time. The Greek's first encounter with the late King Darius ended with the King fleeing for his life.

"I am concerned." General Theodore said, breaking the silence. He was a tall, rangy man in his late twenties with a powerful intellect and bright green eyes that twinkled with alert intelligence. General Edward accompanied him. The two distinguished generals rode on a frail mountainous road from Patra to Athens on miniature-breed Skyrian horses. These were not war horses but friendly, unsodden, perfect for climbing the metropolis. The men were en route to a Demokratia meeting, where people gathered to voice their opinions and arguments.

"What seems to be ailing you?" asked Edward, a tall, muscular man who stood like he could carry the world on his shoulders. They were two generals assigned to oversee the city-states' external affairs. In theory, these assemblies were supposed to unite all Greek citizens. General Edward thought these meetings consumed much time, which could have been spent exercising.

"I have been thinking," said Theodore. "And when are you not thinking?" humored Edward. Theodore's mind was overactive and preoccupied, especially before meetings. When they arrived, thousands of representatives from various city-states were present. The official gatherings were held in a vast building called a Prytaneion, a religious and political center in the community, on a hill in front of the Acropolis, a place expressly prepared for the event. Fifty prytaneis, executives in power, stood on platforms carved into the rock. On the first platform were the secretaries and scribes. In the second step was the orators. Sometimes, these sessions lasted from dawn to dusk. Forty times a year, they gather to propose laws, decrees, and projects. This was the first part of a long negotiating practice before it was sent to the Council of the Boule for more consideration.

The generals dismounted their horses and proceeded to the meeting. "The Persians," replied Theodore thoughtfully after considerable time. "The war is not over, and it must continue. The subjugated Greeks of Asia have not been liberated yet, and we must not forget our pledge to them." He was not supposed to fear, but deep inside, he was petrified of the Persians, and with good reason.

"What makes you think the Persians will campaign against us again? I hear the King is having women problems," Edward said, laughing out loud. He was glad women were not allowed to attend public meetings; in his mind, they were deceitful, savage, sexually insatiable, and frivolous gossipers.

"It will be a matter of time before they strike again," Theodore said, looking at a Magpie flying over them, birds associated with magic and fortune-telling from the underworld. "The Persians are relentless barbarians that would not stop trying to invade us; we must be prepared."

General Theodore was not from the distinguished people of Athens; his mother was half-Greek, and he did not have freemen's rights, nor could he own land. He grew up vehemently impetuous with quick apprehension, action, and a lavish style, constantly creating arguments by excusing or accusing others of something perceived as unfair. Theodore used oration skills for a declaration to defend his view. His teachers thought he would be destined to do great or evil things because he lacked self-correction and did not adhere to sound advice regarding his behavior or mannerisms. However, he excelled in management affairs and philosophy, developing a political shrewdness inspired by Solon.

"The leaders think it is over after the Battle of Marathon, but I think it's just the beginning of our sorrows," said Theodore. "This is why I continue to train my soldiers and prepare the city for the invasion." He was going to make a proposal and needed to convince Edward to support him.

"I have a proposal I want to present to the council today, Edward, and I hope you back me up on this." Edward was mild and nobler in public matters, not acting for self-interest or popularity but for the state's best interest. On many occasions, he disagreed with Theodore. "Let's hear what you are proposing, Theodore; I know what an enterprising man you are, and sometimes we do not have the same views, but I am willing to listen and give you an opinion before you present it to the council," replied Edward.

Edward also had concerns regarding the security of the sea. Specifically, The Mediterranean Sea. The central superhighway of transport, trade, and cultural exchange between three continents.

Meanwhile, in the Zagros mountains, Zenia was beyond herself. In the royal palace, damsels were assigned to the royal nursery to care for the children, so Zenia did not know what to do when the baby woke up crying. She tried to comfort him, but she knew he was hungry. It had been hours since he had his last feeding.

Thoughts of the baby's mother rose in her mind. Who was she, and what was she doing in a lion's den, birthing a child alone? Zenia supposed the mother was dead and could not ignore the child's cries. She cringed at the thought of the lion returning to the den and consuming the child. Zenia was full of compassion for the babe. It was still several hours before Zenia would arrive at Sippar. Desperately, she looked through her food: figs, oats, bread, nothing for a newborn. How long will he live without food?

Poor babe, she thought. She had delivered him from the mouth of the lion but feared she would be unable to deliver him from the jaws of hunger. The tiny bundle in her arms waved his little clenched fist in protest, demanding food. His wrinkled red face, toothless mouth, and little bald head reminded her of a miniature king.

Zenia stroked the baby, feeling helpless. What was she going to do? Was there a God that could deliver? The baby's cries tugged at her heartstrings; tears of frustration filled her eyes. Giving the baby a little water might help get him back to sleep, but how would she feed the baby water? She was reminded of Hagar, a story about a poor Egyptian woman who was left to die in the wilderness with a hungry child. "Oh, if only an angel would appear to me with milk," she pleaded. "Then I also can trust in the God of heaven." But no such thing happened. Then, finally, she did get an idea. Quickly, she pulled out a clean piece of cloth from her travel kit and soaked oats in water. Then, she twisted the fabric in a spiral, dipped the corner into the soaking liquid, and then put the cloth to the baby's mouth. The baby opened its mouth, sucked on the fabric, and swallowed. It was a slow process, but the baby got full and returned to sleep.

Zenia was exhausted when she arrived at Sippar that evening, but her mind was alert. Norman her uncle greeted her at the door. He was the keeper of her inn and was pleasantly surprised to see Zenia but wondered about the child in her arms. Zenia faked faintly, falling into his arms. "Quickly, Naomi," he called. "Come, the Queen is faint and with a child!" Naomi appeared from behind a curtain. "What is all the commotion?" she asked. "Get a chair, Naomi," Norman said. After Zenia was seated, Norman took the baby from her arms. The baby woke up, piercing the air with screeching cries, adding to the drama. "My baby needs suckling," Zenia said, limping as if she was losing consciousness. Naomi had fetched a helper to get a wet nurse from the town in less than ten minutes.

CHAPTER EIGHT

THE ROYAL HAREM

The late King Cyrus was a controversial king. After he captured Babylon, he allowed the Hebrews to return to their land, build their walls, and rebuild the temple of the Hebrew God, which King Nebuchadnezzar had destroyed. Materials, resources, and even slave workers were provided to help them. He even returned the gold and silver vessels taken to Babylon. Many rejoiced and returned home, including the prophets. However, Amara's Uncle Kaleb's family stayed behind because they had prospered in the foreign land, and building the temple of God became less important. Some believed King Cyrus extended special treatment to the Hebrews for leaving the city gates open so he could march into Babylon and seize it.

Amara was one of the virgins in the Achaemenid Empire, sanctioned to appear in the Shushan Palace. The damsel was a slender cypress with a face brighter than the sun and lips like pomegranate flowers. In his eagerness to get her into the royal harem, Uncle Kaleb entered the women's house, where only the King was allowed. Mother Queen Adi was angry when she found him and dismissed him from the King's inner courts. He was put outside in front of the palace as a tower guard. Amara's heart was nettled with anguish, for she yearned to return home.

Adi, Mother Queen, Shah's mother, was a vain, dominant, and cunning woman, but she knew how to appoint subjects to benefit herself best. She assigned Rosie as the King's chamberlain and keeper of the women to ensure the young maidens were accommodated, adequately trained, and purified before they were presented to the King.

Rosie took the royal ladies for a tour of the royal harem. It was a spacious L-shaped structure with room for expansion. The central hub was oriented north to south. The west wing extended westward from the southern portion of the main wing. The center of the main branch was a large hall columned with a portico facing a spacious courtyard on the north. The doorway had four doors. On the jambs of the southern entrance, King Dawit was depicted entering the hall, followed by two attendants. One carried a fly whisk, and the other held a parasol over the King's head. In the eastern doorway, a relief showed Dawit fighting a lion-headed monster. Reliefs on the western exit showed the King in combat with a lion. The Queen's quarters were reserved for her and her entourage in the central section of the palace. South of the columned hall, there were six apartments arranged in two rows. Each apartment had a large, pillared room and two smaller rooms. The west wing contained sixteen additional apartments.

The rooms were decorated with curtains made of brocade material. Lushes' carpets, hand-woven carpets made of wool and silk, covered the floors. They had patterns of ornaments in elaborate spirals and tendrils called infinite repeat. This was said to protect the owner from bad luck and misfortune. The air was perfumed with musk, ambergris, and flowers. Ambergris was also used for medicine and spices from sperm whales.

Access from the Council Hall to the northern part of the harem's main wing was two stairways connecting the west wing with the Palace of Dawit. There were also two exits to enclosed gardens. A third exit at the eastern end of the western wing led to an accessible area. Everything had to be perfect for the royal concubines.

"Thou servant has done well," said Mother Queen to Rosie, her devoted servant. "Thy slaves will neither rest nor slumber until the royal maidens become the footstool to thy Shah's feet," answered Rosie. Mother Queen had very high standards for her devotees, and the young virgins will soon find out. She returned to the large hall where the virgins were gathered. The room was full of exhilaration and apprehension, but they became quiet as soon as she entered. The only sounds came from outside, from the howling of the fiercest southern winds.

"Thy maidens begin purification early in the morn, for the turning of the six lunars," Mother Queen divulged, her eyes like ice. She paused, waiting for protest. The comprehensively bushy-tail ladies stood silent; no one dared to make a sound. "After that cycle, six more lunars for beautification," continued Mother Queen. This sprung mouths to whisper, murmur, and grumble. The girls had no idea what to expect; they all came from different backgrounds, and each had their rituals, but some thought twelve lunar months was a long time for purification, especially Amara, who wanted to hide under a rock.

"Hezar damsels," whispered Vanessa to Amara. "What city doth thy comes from?" she asked, with an accent. Amara whispered back, "Susa."

"I come from Mesopotamia, the city of Akkad," Vanessa offered. She was friendly and had reservations about being at the palace, but her father was a high-ranking official in their province, and she was sent to represent him.

Some virgins thought the twelve-month period was an induction period to enculturate them. Amara wondered if they would change her name. Others were shocked, thinking it was a long preparation. Little did they know that not all would be chosen to go before the King, even after the twelve-month purification.

Amara thought the palace had rigid standards and worried. First, she had to be healthy, with physical strength and a strong mind. Her skin had to be without blemishes, and Amara had a drachma-sized mole on the small part of her spine. Secondly, she would have a hymen check, and non-virgins were prohibited. Thirdly, her body had to be firm like a fish, with comely cheeks, breasts like abhattikhim, eyes like a dove, and lips like pomegranate flowers. Her belly had to be shaped like a quince. But most importantly, she had to be fertile, like a well-watered field bearing many fruits.

There were mixed emotions on the faces of the young women, some of whom were not yet fourteen. Several girls were apprehensive, and others just wanted to go home, for they had left family, friends, and suitors to participate in what they thought was a beauty contest. Some delighted in the opportunity to obtain power; they romanticized being deflowered by the King and possibly becoming the Queen of Persia.

Clearing her voice and raising her right hand, Mother Queen got the ladies' attention. The room went silent. "My servant, Dr. Democedes, will check for infirmities and blemishes. My maidservant Rosie will take thee to the hammam for cleansing and fresh coverings."

Democedes was a Greek physician who had fallen into the clutches of the Lydian satrap and was sent as a captive to Susa. Like the sky, he was a stunning, muscular man with sage hair, an ivory complexion, and bright blue eyes. He was the renowned royal Doctor, having healed Mother Queen from a lump on her breast, which the Egyptian physicians could not treat. Dr. Democedes was the first empirical physician in the Persian court.

He lived in luxury but longed to return to Greece, where his people were in chaos, but was denied. Democedes was not a eunuch, but he was a trusted man of the King, allowed to examine the royal harem under the ever-watching eyes of Mother Queen.

"Rosie, separate the women in hundreds," ordered Mother Queen. Rosie wasted no time; in a flash, she had the ladies lined up and ready to be medically examined.

Amara was going through the motions, but deep inside, she was shattered. How can her uncle do this to her? How could she send messengers to Todd? Could he help her? She had not stopped thinking of him.

"Your head is much more valuable than whatever it may be," Amara heard a male saying. It was the Eunuch. Apologetically, she bowed, forced a smile, and admitted, "I am anxious with thoughts."

"Each day has enough trouble of its own; worry, not," said Haggai, walking away.

The harem's lifestyle was not discussed publicly, so Amara fantasized they were likened to brothel-style sexual playgrounds filled with beautiful, glistening women lounging around steam baths. But that was only a half-truth. The women, both legal-marriage wives and concubines, were relied upon for reproduction. These ladies were subject only to the King. The harem was a fine-tuned specialized hierarchy that allowed the ladies to function most productively. The King could have as many wives and concubines as he could afford, increasing the royal expenses. Each girl was given a living quarter, fine clothing, jewelry, a spending allowance, a dowry, estates, and many servants, including eunuchs. The women were separated into three groups.

First were the household women, legal wives other than the Queen or the mistress. Unmarried princesses and married girls lived with their own families. Then there were the beautiful girls bought in slave markets, received as gifts, or collected from different parts of the empire, like Zenia, the Queen, to be replaced.

The women were royal and aristocratic and received an arduous education. Some learned skills such as horsemanship, archery, and hunting. Others appeared publicly and traveled with the King to participate in feasts in vast estates and entertainment.

Some, like Zenia, employed many servants and professional laborers, wielding political power. The women were equivalent to royal estates and could be used as tokens for gifts to honorary men, married for the annexation and expansion of the dynasty, or sold for the right price.

Mother Queen was at the highest level of the harem, empowered by the King to maintain order and productivity. She ensured Shah's sons learned about politics and had acceptable social behaviors.

Karins were the favorite women of the King and usually possessed extraordinary beauty. They were trained in various skills, such as singing, dancing, and music. Often, male guests of the kingdom would be presented with an Odalisque, female slaves, to keep them company in the evening. Many women throughout the harem sought to obtain any of the levels in the women's house; doing so ensured that they would be provided for and got a rank and position that would give them the best life they could dream of.

Only eunuchs were allowed around the royal ladies. Castrated before puberty and molded for a life of servitude, eunuchs provided their services to King Dawit with peace of mind. Rendered sexless, these men were ideal guards to watch over beautiful women. Some would have carnal desires, but the fear of losing their heads kept them pure. Like harem women, there were hierarchies among the eunuchs; some had more power than others. The commander of the eunuchs could approach the King at any time, arrange special events such as births and weddings, and promote and demote the women of the harem. He even had the power to order a woman's execution if he believed she deserved it.

This was Amara's new home, and she was miserable.

CHAPTER NINE

RUMORS OF WAR

A long and heated council meeting had the men in the gymnasium highly upset. The generals supported the vote on General Theodore's proposal to utilize the silver to build more fleets. Some were not happy. They did not believe spending more silver on a fleet was necessary to fight a battle that might never happen. Others wished that Theodore would leave them alone; they were trying to prepare for the Olympic competitions.

Not all who frequented the gymnasium were there to work out or socialize; some were there to drop an ear and listen to the latest reports. The Persians planted well-paid tyrants in the city-states, keeping the King well-informed.

No one suspected these traitors, for some, were high-ranking officers within the military leadership. Theodore, however, did not have the wool pulled over his eyes. Like his nemesis Edward, he naturally suspected anyone who spoke any of the three Persian main languages.

"It has been almost eight years since the late King Darius was forced to retreat in the Battle of Marathon," said Theodore. "But that does not mean the war is over." He looked around at the other generals, who were uninterested in discussing war. Instead, they were more interested in relaxing, drinking, and wrestling. "Our most populous and wealthy cities on the western coast of Anatolia are still under Persian control," continued Theodore, ignoring their indifference. "Greece had fought hard and furiously to earn its independence," interjected General Edward, "the Persians have learned their lesson."

"We continue to develop, spreading everywhere, and sooner or later, we will conflict with Persia and their vassal states. I am not comfortable with the quiet before the storm. They must be regrouping," said King Leonidas, General of Sparta. "I agree with General Theodore; the war is not over."

"Men, men, it has been eight years!" spoke General Edward of Corinth. "I don't think King Dawit has the same passion as his father. The war is over, and western Anatolia has enough wealth to protect its borders." He looked around to see who agreed with him. Some did, but the majority did not.

"What are you saying?" asked General Theodore, standing up. His chiseled body glistened. "We must never forget how Persia reacted to the Ionian revolts. For years, they have used tyrants to divide and conquer! Aristagoras was an excellent example. He started the Ionian revolt to serve his selfish purpose." More men around the Gymnasium gathered to listen to the discussion.n.

"Releasing the wrath of Persia upon us." Said General Cimon, a three-time Olympics winner. He looked at Theodore hard. "Athens and Eretria, two impetuous cities, provoking the demons of Persia," he said with his bright eyes large with indignation. "Athens was helping a sister city and should not be at fault," replied General Theodore. "We need not focus on past mistakes but look forward and prepare for the storm that wavers our way."

Theodore was in an argumentative mood, "We must credit the Ionians who fought hard, blood, sweat, and tears, against the enormous Army of the beast." His childhood fears reminded him of the Ionia battles, and he remembered how he cheered them for standing up against the massive army. A mischievous smile crossed Theodore's face, "Let me remind you of Athens' courage, how they marched toward the capital of Sardis, sieged it, and burned it down to the ground as a burnt offering to Cybele, the goddess of the earth."

"But the Persians regrouped and headed straight for the snake's head, Miletus. We thought they were retreating and were surprised at the Battle of Lade, where they defeated the Ionian fleet. If we had not been crossed by the Samians, cowards who fled in the middle of the battle, leaving the Ionians stranded without backup, the three years of fighting would not have been in vain, and today, we would be celebrating their glorious victory, said another general.

"And Miletus was sieged, and all males killed, women and children enslaved, and the city destroyed," cried Theodore indignantly, stirring up rumbling and protest from the spectators.

Theodore could feel his ears turning hot with anger. When the Persians strike again, and he knows they will, who will be his allies? He wondered; would he also be abandoned in the heat of the battle?

"We must reinforce our battle strategies," said Theodore. "The proposal made to the council of the Boule to use the money from the silver of the Laurium mines to finance a navy will prepare us."

The gymnasium suddenly went silent; the silver money was divided among themselves, and many lost monies they could use for personal use, but it made perfect sense to build a fleet. "This gift from Zeus is to help us," Theodore exhorted. It was Theodore's foresight, but the people of Athens needed to be more trusted of other Greeks, for many had questions about who would be in charge of the fleet. The reality was that the city-states of Greece were in turmoil, weak, scattered, and not united, and they would be unable to stand against the monstrous Persia without military power. "A house divided will not stand," Theodore said, "but together as brothers, we can secure the future of Greece, and two hundred triremes is a gift from Mighty Zeus."

King Dawit, the mighty, sat on the throne of Persia as the master of the world. He was the honored Shah, but evil men waxed by envy sought ways to inflict his soul. Lust for his wife, Queen Zenia, never wholly ceased to afflict him, and other things eventually became less critical to King Dawit. On rare occasions when his mind and body were idle, the emptiness in his heart hurt like an incision that never healed. He had no peace, and his passion had shivered like wheat in the heat.

Gabe sat outside the King's chambers; he was Shah's bodyguard. When King Dawit was strong, he shined like the Sun, but he would wax like the Moon when the evil eye glanced at him. The evil eye was upon him on this day, and he had taken to bed with a heavy spirit. The King did not want the magicians, astrologers, or naysayers to be called. He thought their smoke and mirrors were vanities of vanities that profited him nothing. Concerned for the Shah, Gabe called for Mother Queen. King Dawit would welcome a visit from his mother, for he deeply loved her.

Mother Queen wasted no time when she heard her beloved son had taken to bed. She immediately called the Magi to sacrifice a sheep and interpret the liver for signs. The priest could then tell her the diagnosis and necessary rituals to relieve her son from the daevas that afflicted him.

The high priest scrutinized the sheep's liver. He believed the liver was the source of blood and life itself. The baru was specially trained to interpret the signs of the liver. First, he divided the organs into sections representing different deities. Then, he made a clay model to study the specimen.

"Aka Manah has afflicted with the Shah," said the Magi, looking up from the model. "Ahriman was sent to seduce the King's evil mind, purpose, thinking, and intention of sensual desires."

"I pray thee bring up the Shah, nourish him for the kingdom, aid him with thy might and mind," Queen Mother supplicated on bended knees. "O thou eternally and good, O source of happiness, incline thine ear unto me and listen to my voice. If my son has sinned and strayed in Ahriman's paths, behold his repentance, and pardon him. My soul is heavy; my heart is fearful for the reason of my child, for will not the nobles say this king presageth evil? They will hold me up to shame, and how can I reply to their questions? It behooves me to remove this affliction that the land of Persia is not accursed."

The Magi made a talisman, a prayer on animal skin rolled in a small gold case decorated with a lapis lazuli stone forming an eye to protect the King against the evil spirit, and gave it to Mother Queen. In haste and anxious to apply the remedy, Mother Queen left and did not hear the last part of the liver reading: "And when the day had torn the folds of night asunder, the two armies met in battle, and the fight waged strong until the setting of the Sun. And the earth was a sea of blood."

Then Mother Queen prepared a savory stew and some cakes; she put the bread in a basket, put the stew in a pot, brought it to her son, and presented it. "My son, rise and eat, for thy strength is faint, but Vohu Manah will strengthen thee."

King Dawit could smell the spices in the stew; his hunger awakened, and he sat up. "Seeing your face is like the face of an angel," he said with a smile.

"May the Lord keep and guard thee. May thine enemies be utterly destroyed. May the days of Shah the Great be happy, for the Almighty hath accomplished his desire. He hath given me a son born unto the mighty warrior behind the curtains of his house, a moon-faced boy, beautiful of face and limb, in whom there is neither fault nor blemish," said Mother Queen as she bowed unto the earth in homage. Then Dawit sat up and ate, and his spirit was strengthened, but he refused the wine, for his fearful heart did not want his mind to wander, forgetting his deeds and actions.

"My son," Mother Queen said after her son was full and merry. "Listen to what I say. The operation in the harem is flourishing like the Cypress trees of Lebanon."

"And the numbers of the servants?" Dawit asked with interest.

"Two hundredfold," replied Queen Mother. "The most beautiful of all the land, full of grace," she smiled. The face of Dawit lit up like the Sun after the fog, and his heart leaped for joy. "Cast vain imaginations of Zenia out of thy mind. Preserve thy strength and passion for the comely virgins being purified for thy pleasure, my son. Rise from thy bed, face the Sun, and present thyself to Ahura Mazda the all-wise."

King Dawit listened to his wise mother and was in high spirits when Gabe knocked on the door. "Shah, Artabanus requested a visit with thee."

A NEWBORN KING

Zenia had arrived at Sippar late in the evening, tired, hungry, and dirty, but with a little bundle of joy she had delivered from sure death. Sippar was near Eastern Sumerian, a Babylonian city on the Euphrates River's east bank, where Zenia had a well-established operation manufacturing military uniforms. Many of the land's inhabitants were hired servants who produced wool, and others were scribes. There was a school for boys, an e-dubba, and a tablet house where they would spend years learning to read and write the cuneiform script. After graduation, the throne employed them as dubsars or tablet writers.

When the midwife arrived, Zenia enjoyed a bowl of sherbet with Kachee. The baby lay next to her, fast asleep. It was amazing how quickly she was recovering from childbirth, thought Naomi, whose births were not easy, and healing was a slow process. Naomi wondered why Zenia was traveling without a maidservant, especially in late pregnancy and on horseback.

Naomi had known Zenia since she was a child and worried about her when she had been taken to Susa by the late Darius. Never in her life would she have envisioned Zenia becoming a subservient queen. As a young girl, she was unwavering, stubborn, and tenacious. It was not a big surprise to anyone when she was dethroned. Despite what anyone said, Zenia did the correct thing when she refused to parade naked before a group of drunken men. Naomi was appalled. She did not know the King had dismissed his wife while carrying their first son. That was disturbing.

Dani was a tall, pretty girl with large brown eyes and sandy brown hair, a Chaldean. She was an excellent midwife with wisdom in treating childbirth. The medicine of the Medes and Persians was the same as the Chaldeans. In the tradition, everything that manifested power or growth was alive, a particular demon. If a woman suffered from gynecological problems, it was a daeva pictured as a horrible monster with swine sucking at her breast. This spirit was responsible for the death of infants, children, and women in childbirth. The cure was simple: antitoxins of primitive medicine, chants, and rituals. The ceremonies symbolized the afflicted destroying and being released from the grasp of the daevas. Behind every sickness were daevas and a specific ritual to remove them.

"Queen Zenia lives forever," said Dani. "Blessed are ye in all the Kingdom. My heart rejoices in your presence, my Queen." She bowed to the ground in reverence. Zenia extended her hand toward her to be kissed. Some rituals had to be performed before and after childbirth that Zenia knew nothing about. God had redeemed her barren womb through a surrogate for the mistreatment of the King. The child was a gift from God in her mind.

"The babe," said Zenia, suffered much with hard labor, as I suffered bearing and protecting him from King Dawit, who conspired against me. Waste not thy time on me, my servant, but see to the child, for I fear the umbilical cord was severed.

Dani turned her attention to the little bundle, fast asleep, wrapped in a white cotton blanket. The child had not been ceremonially cleansed, and Dani could see it was covered in dry amniotic fluid. Gently, she reached out a hand and tentatively lifted a corner of the blanket. The little pink face was sound asleep. Unwrapping the babe more, she saw tiny, fragile shoulders, waving arms, and tight fists. She carefully inspected the stump of the umbilical cord, which had a hairpin hanging from it. It was disgusting. It was not natural; the wound was infected. She pulled the blanket farther down, "It's a male child," she announced excitedly. Having a child was a blessing, but having a male was double the blessing and praiseworthy.

The men outside the room rejoiced when they heard the child was a male. "A new king is born," roused Norman with his face of a proud Abba—time to celebrate. "Quickly, fetch a young fatted calf for the sacrifice," he told a shepherd boy who came to greet the Queen. "Norman, have the boy bring the uterus of the lamb," called Naomi from behind the door.

"The uterus?" Norman bemused. "Why, my wife? That is a strange request." Naomi stuck her head from behind the curtain in the room, "For the cleansing, my husband."

"Ah, women stuff," he laughed, "the way of a maid with a man who can understand?" The men with him gather around him, rejoicing and celebrating.

"The babe has a minor infection," Dani announced. "I have herbs for that. Thy child is a beautiful male, perfect in form, with strong limbs and the heart of a lion." Zenia thought about the lion, who appeared to her while exiting the den with the babe strapped on her back. Was the child a prophet? She wondered if men and beasts from all parts of the earth would come to give homage. These things she hid in her heart.

Dani busied herself, cleaning the screaming babe. Meanwhile, Naomi and the house servants gathered items for the newborn. The belly button was tied with two pieces of blue and white colored threads. The babe was cleansed and dressed in a long white cotton dress called a 'peerahan e ghiyamat,' meaning resurrection. Diapers were put on next, and the babe was dressed in a shirt on top and placed in a ghondagh, all in white. His bald little head was covered with a small hat. Dani prepared pieces of butter with crystallized sugar dissolved in warm water and fed it to the baby, which the babe drank like he had not been fed in hours.

"The first six days are important, my lady," Dani explained to Zenia. "Evil and darkness will try to attack you and the babe, but I will be here to prove against them." Then Dani burned incense and blew it toward the baby and the mother in six directions. She took some of the ashes and put a beauty mark on Zenia's eyebrows, palms, breasts, and feet. The aroma of espand and camphor filled the house. The babe's eyes were darkened with the ashes, which he vigorously protested.

News traveled fast in Babylon. Many came to pay homage to the royal babe on the sixth day, but Zenia had not yet thought of a name for her son. A carpenter made a rocking bed, and his wife decorated it with quilts, pillows, and sheaths. One of the female priestesses made a talisman for his health and protection and to ward off evil daevas. Some brought soap, cleaning powder, and herbal medicine. Still, others gave espand, camphor, powder, and nabat. Families with significant wealth presented the baby with elaborate seismooney, herbs, clothing, diapers, hats, toys, precious stones, gold, and silver. The people greatly adored Zenia, and they loved the royal baby.

Norman and Naomi prepared the celebration on the sixth day to name the babe. They invited the local Magi, Gaspar. Before dinner, the babe was brought to this man. The Magi was a tall, mysterious-looking man with sharp eyes and a sword strapped to his waist. He took the babe into his arms. He looked at the innocent child, kissed his brows, and lifted him to the heavens. "There arises one named Iskandar; thy throne shall be a symbol of a sixteen-ray star, and he shall rule with horns of Ammon. He shall scatter the world's kingdoms to the four winds."

The honored guest broke out in celebration. When all were merry with joy, Zenia approached the Magi, "Tell unto me, I pray thee, for thou hast might and wisdom, should I remain thus ever satisfied, for surely not unto the throne of Persia?" asked Zenia.

The wise Magi did not want to worry Queen Zenia. She had been through so much; the prophecy was for the uncertain future. He thought she could focus on raising the child with wisdom and understanding. "Bewildered not thyself in the unknown for no one knows, but he who experiences the mysterious future," he told her. "Oh, wise one, bewildered already I am, for wicked men could do wicked to avert serendipity. For good hast thou done, and injustice dost lead, for my husband's heart has turned cold through trickery and lies, dismissed me for no fault. But the face of God thus shines upon my quandary, and thy servant has been blessed with a male child."

"Then shall be watered with blood the leaves and fruits of the tree spring from the vengeance that is due. For unto this day hath vengeance slumbered, but now is there sprung a branch from the tree which the enemy uprooted, and he shall come as a raging lion, girt with a vengeance," replied the Magi.

The Magi called for the scroll where stars were written, and he searched for the planets of the lad. He found that Jupiter reigned in the sign of the Archer in the house of Iskandar and the sun in the lion in the seventh house. And when he saw this, he was joyful, for he knew Iskandar would be blessed and strong. Then, having read the secrets of Fate, the Magi blessed the child and his mother. Before he departed, he cautioned Norman, "appoint high-ranking eunuchs in the King's service to nurture the child, not at the hands of a low-born female nurse. They are schooled to make him handsome by massaging his limbs into the correct shape."

Days after the celebration, outraged, the men in Babylon rallied. Then they prepared their arms, and the number of men was great. Helmets were joined to helmet, spear to spear, and elephants without number went with them, and you would have said it was a host that none could understand. And they marched, their hearts filled with rage for what the evil King had done to the Queen. The protest could be heard from miles away. Many came from neighboring cities to discover the outcry, but a wise man stood up and spoke. He was like water to a burning fire.

"What King Dawit had done, removed the Queen and the throne's heir, is an outrage, but we must be wise and vigilant, not stirring up commotions that would bring wrath upon us. Let us consult together quietly and peacefully. What ye sow, ye reaps. Let us sow into an army and prepare our minds and body with the sternness of an athlete for a great fight, for unto us a King was born."

CHAPTER ELEVEN

MARDUK- GOD OF STORMS

Gaia watched from his mud-brick home as the erosive winds uprooted weeds and anything not profoundly grounded. Gaia, the High Priest of Marduk, was having difficulty sleeping. The intense storms contrasted with his preparation plans for the Feist of Akitu. It was the time of year in Babylon when day turned to night with many sandstorms approaching. More people would volunteer in fine weather, but when the new moon rose, the city was engulfed by a dust wall that stretched from the sky onward, casting a bleak dark curtain on his plans. Any outdoor activities requiring physical labor were stopped. He returned to his bed and lay awake, listening desolately to the howling of the winds. He felt he had prayed enough and wondered if Marduk had heard him.

The winds exceeding sixty miles per hour were typical for that time of year. The violent winds uprooted trees, collapsed homes, and killed people and animals. Was Marduk causing the enveloping winds to cripple the city of Sippar?

In the previous week, every temple priest was sent to speak to the viziers and priestesses of the market towns. They told them it was time to obtain forgiveness, return what had been borrowed, pay their debts, bring gifts to the temple, and give alms to the poor. They could receive forgiveness for their sins by working in the temple every fourth day of the week, preparing for the Feist of Akitu. If they helped clean the Ésagila Temple, they would get forgiveness for the past year's sins. In addition, a day of labor was worth a week of routine sins, excluding sacrilege and murders.

Gaia himself went to Mesopotamia and spoke in fifteen of the thirty-two ziggurats. He had three priests with him and sent two others to Susa.

The people would make the trip for their annual celebrations. Thousands of people had heard the message.

There was no way of estimating how many might respond or, if any, would.

Annually, the Ésagila Temple was scrubbed, dusted, and polished. Marduk's silver and gold idol watched as the people cleaned walls, floors, and relics for the twelve-day Spring ceremony in his honor. He was the patron god of Babylon, the King of the Gods, the judge of justice, the compassionate healer, and the originator of magic. Most importantly, he was the God of the harvest and the storms, the blesser of the seeds.

Good weather would help to achieve most of the work. Would anyone come with the massive plume of dust and sand blown by the winds from the desert? The dust clouds were so thick that all living creatures had to be sheltered to avoid suffocation. Herdsmen were busy with their livestock, and volunteering was not a priority.

Gaia sat up. It was darker outside, and he had virtually no visibility as the slow-moving sandstorm continued to approach. The sounds of flying objects clashing in the wind continued to intensify. King Dawit had not been attending the annual celebrations.

Each year, the storms were escalating more furiously. The presence of the King was essential to the festivities, to honor the rebirth of the natural world. The ferocious wind roared like a lion, uprooting anything ungrounded. Babylon was vulnerable because King Dawit had failed in his role, causing relentless dust storms in the Winter months and floods in the Spring.

At midnight, Gaia got up. He was unable to go back to sleep.

He sat thinking of the decline of Babylon. The High Priest believed caring for people was the service of God. He had trouble focusing on the prospects of the days ahead. What kind of man did the people regard King Dawit to be? A master of deception, consumed by wine that could never equal his father. He did not care for those who depended on him for support and protection. King Dawit did not care for the people the way his father had. He could not be the representative of Marduk. Gaia believed there was an afterlife where the souls of men, even the souls of Kings, were balanced.

At last, dawn cracked, and the veil lifted, but it was still dark. Gaia covered his body from head to toe in a hooded robe to protect his skin from being ripped apart as he walked against the winds toward the temple. He entered an elaborately designed ziggurat decorated in stair step style, ascending to a point where Marduk dwelled, and only special priests were allowed. The fast-moving hot air flurried in a consuming vortex that could lift a camel from the ground as it moved. He walked faster to avoid flying particles. The wind slammed the heavy door behind him as a tree came crashing down, missing him by a split second.

Gaia and his officials had arranged for a meeting at the Ésagila Temple to discuss their progress.

He feared the weather would interfere with the plans. He was wrong. All were waiting in the meeting room. Jamal, a short, round man with a giant schnoz, the temple treasurer; Shamash, a tall Babylonian wearing a turban, a city official; and other temple priests and priestesses. They all had concerned looks on their faces. One of the servants entered the room with a hot pot of savory goat stew.

The room was lit with the fresh aromas of bread, herbs, and spices. The smells reminded Gaia that he was famished.

Pottery vessels, with a linen wick dosed in olive oil, and four spouts lit the room. The guests sat on floor mats around a large table for breakfast. Gaia dipped a piece of flatbread in the goat stew. He savored each bite and gulped goat's milk, licking his fingers. He loved food and smacked his lips as he reached for more goat stew and cucumber salad. They ate silently because chatting during the meal would invite evil spirits.

Norman, 57, cousin of Queen Zenia, entered the room, his face covered with a woolen balaclava.

The wind slammed the door behind him.

Quietly, he removed his dusty cloak and sat down. He paused briefly in prayer, gave reverence, and wiped his hands and face with a wet cloth before he started eating. He looked agitated. Gaia had been waiting to get an update on Zenia's return. Typically, she would attend the meeting. She was currently completing the forty-day after-birth ritual.

He wanted to know more about her removal as the Queen of Persia. This could significantly impact the temple's finances, which the King had already reduced.

"Has thy heard the news of morn?" Norman asked as soon as the plates were removed from the table. No one in the room answered, mesmerized by the shadows cast by the flickering of the oil lamps and listening to the howling and crashing sounds outside. An uncertain future was warring against the wind.

"King Dawit will not attend the Feast of Akitu," announced Norman. The sounds of disbelief echoed around the temple. Gaia got up like a haboob storm, thunder and lightning coming out of his eyes. He was not one given to anger, but as the administrator of Marduk, he had every reason to be upset. King Dawit knew the Spring Celebration was essential for the Babylonians' future.

Discordant talk rumbled around the room, with protests being spoken by the priests and priestesses.

"What excuse has the King offered this time?" Gaia asked with his voice modulated for control. He did not want to raise evil spirits in their midst. His face was flushed with anger. The sounds of swirling, gusting winds intensified outside.

A young, rambunctious priest in a brown tunic could no longer stay quiet. "Since King Dawit has ascended to the throne, he has failed to attend the New Year's annual celebration." He was a twenty-year-old Greek eunuch, an exile from Chios. He did not choose to become a priest, just as his sister did not choose to be taken to the royal harem. King Dawit had him clean-shaved and enslaved his sister in the royal harem.

"The feast is a twelve-day yearly celebration on the first full moon of the Vernal Equinox. The only time the arrogant King is humbled before God," the young priest continued, venting in frustration. He was not the only one frustrated. "The King offered no excuse," answered Norman. His face was red with outrage. He did not speak quietly. He did not care if he woke the spirits; they needed to be awakened.

"The world has darkened," said Gaia. "Does the King think he is above God? The King has been gifted with fortune, cavalry, infantry, and fleets of ships, gold, silver, and women. He is never satisfied but continues to indulge his heart with youthful passion."

"The King dares to defile Marduk, for his worship is to another, and a house divided cannot stand.

He has forgotten that God gives life on earth for all, including him," said Shamash-Eriba indignantly. "This is not the first time he has offended us.

When will we take the lead and march against King Dawit?" continued Shamash-Eriba, his voice getting louder as the winds blew harder. Loud crashes outside the temple increased as loose debris knocked against the stone building. One of the priestesses screamed when a gust of wind blew the door open, and earth came gushing into the room. A young priest closed the door, but the lamp oils had blown out. This was too much for everyone.

"The King is a man of flesh and blood who causes us to tremble for fear of punishment. Should we continue to obey a man who defiles God?" asked Norman in the darkness. "The fields have not yielded a hundredfold since his reign, and why? Because he has not humbled himself before God!"

"Gak! Cursed is the land that does not honor God; this is blaspheme," said another priest.

BLASPHEME! The word echoed in the darkness. "Justice had not spread over the land, and the world was better before his reign. The King assesses us with unfair taxes and wants to draw riches from our strength," said Jamal.

"Marduk sends the rain that fills the rivers to water the land. To make the land fertile for us to till and reap. Our reaping would be void if he turned his face from us," said a priestess. "This is blasphemed," she called out, tearing her garments. "Marduk is riding his war chariot, throwing spears of wind against us until he is honored."

The disruptive winds continued to increase as the darkness got darker outside. The cries of wild animals echoed from a distance. Lamps cast ugly shadows on the walls as a young priestess went around the room, lighting them again.

Gaia looked at the priests.

He wanted to resolve the concerns peacefully. He thought sometimes the only way to peace was through the sword. He believed that would be the last resort. "Let's express our concerns to the King. Perhaps his heart will be moved to attend the annual celebration," he said somberly.

A scribe prepared a cuneiform to write the message in the King's language. Gaia wanted to ensure the King read the letter, and though he had reason to believe the King did not know how to read, the translation would be straightforward for one of the many translators.

"Oh, wise King, whose throne revolves around heaven, and the world is better for his reign," stated Gaia. "Let it be known that Marduk gave men fire and showed them how to draw it out of the stone, and he taught them how he led the rivers, that they should water the land and make it fertile. Marduk provided all for the land to be tilled and reaped. He divided the beasts, paired them, and gave them names.

When he passed to a brighter life, he left the world a throne of power. You, King Dawit, have been favored and given authority over the earth.

Through your presence, Marduk releases blessings during our annual celebration. We humble ourselves before thee, O' wise King. Fail not thy obligations to the people and do not delay your attendance at the annual festival. Do not withhold thy blessings from heaven to your humble servants."

Outside, the winds whooshed, scurrying a tower of dust. The howling sounds lashed at the temple walls.

"Is there more to be added?" he asked.

They agreed that all had been said.

"As soon as the storm passes, send a messenger to Susa to deliver the message to the King," said Gaia.

Shamash-Eriba, however, was not in agreement. His heart was lifted with indignation. He was dissatisfied. He thought King Dawit was arrogant and did not follow in his father's footsteps as they had participated in their annual celebrations. The prestige and significance of Babylon's influence were scaling back and shattered, as the King did not observe their rituals. He continued to rule from capitals outside of Babylonia. He secretly met with Bel-Shimanni from Borshippa, who was not present at the meeting.

Shamash-Eriba would not wait for the King's reply, for he knew what a pompous fool the King was. "Let's appoint ourselves as Kings over Sippar and the city of Borshippa to lead in the annual rituals," said Shamash-Eriba to Bel-Shimanni.

Bel-Shimanni was a righteous man who did what was right in the eyes of Marduk. He agreed with Shamash-Eriba. He knew the King's presence during the annual celebration was very important, as he physically represented the people during the rituals. Why should the people be denied the blessings from heaven because King Dawit would not humble himself? "Let us find astrologers and naysayers to speak oracles in public to move the hearts of the people and the High Priest so that we may be anointed in the service of Marduk," suggested Shasmash-Eriba.

Now, it spread around the land that the reign of a man who was mighty and terrible to his people had become an offense to Marduk. Omens were spoken against the King. 'There will be an overthrowing of fortresses and the downfall of garrisons. There will be disobedience for goodwill in the land.'

The nobles and influential leaders withdrew their hearts from King Dawit, pleading to Gaia to appoint representatives to stand before Marduk in the annual celebration so they may be blessed and their crops and animals protected from the fearful storms and floods that continued through the Spring into the Summer months.

Gaia feared this would happen. The people would not honor a King who did not honor God. He went into the temple to ask God for direction and protection since King Dawit had abandoned his duties. But before he could hear from God, affluent families of Sippar and Borshippa, who made large donations to the temple, requested that the two leaders be appointed kings of their cities.

CHAPTER TWELVE

AMARA

I t had been a long day for Amara, and although she was tired, she could not sleep. Betrayal was worse than death. Her uncle had betrayed her, leaving a hole in her heart. She thought of her parents. They were probably suffering grief in their graves at the sight of their daughter in a harem. Where was the silver and gold her father left for her dowry? If she could only get her inheritance, she could flee to Zion, where the rest of the family was.

Outside in the dark, jackals howled to the whipping of the blustery winds. Amara whispered in the dark, "God of Abraham, Issac, and Jacob, in my distress, I call for thee, come and chase my fears away. Uncle Kaleb has left me with no protection nor hope of returning home. I put my hope in you."

Amara tried to fail the humiliating process created by the Mother Queen by pretending she could not read.

Haggai knew her. He had been her schoolmaster. She was fluent in three languages. "Use not trickery to beguile," he warned her. "I knew you when you were still a child. I know about your sufferings. Trust in the God of your ancestors. He will guide you."

Other girls did not make it, and no one knew what became of them, but none had returned home. Girls with physical deformities, like Yoko Shun, who had lotus feet, and Harpreet from Indus Valley, who had genital mutilations, were allowed in the harem because they had exceptional talents and would serve as entertainment. They would never be offered to the King for deflowering.

Yoko Shun was an advent dancer in Gongfu. A deadly dance that could cripple an elephant while she elegantly danced with swords.

Mother Queen was impressed with Harpreet, who played a Ravanahatha, making music pleasing to the ear and calming the spirits. Amara also played a stringed harp. Her music captivated the soul, smoothing and delivering the soul from daeva infestations.

Personally, Adi inspected Amara like she was a sheep. From the moment she looked at the damsel, she wanted to test her. "Open your mouth, turn around, bend down, and cough." The probing into her private areas was more than she could stand. It was the most humiliating thing she had ever encountered. What surprised Amara was how intuitive the Mother Queen was. "Are you in love? Thy countenance radiates with the freshness of a woman in love as did Eve before the viper crawled into the garden."

Sleep eventually came.

The following morning, Amara was woken by a knock on her door. At first, she was confused. The surroundings were strange. A sheer curtain surrounded her bed with lavender-scented pillows. Was she dreaming? Even the mattress felt like she was flowing in the air.

Curiously, she had to look under the sheets. It was a goatskin sewn into a bed and filled with water. She remembered that suddenly she was at the Shushan Palace, in the harem.

There was another knock on the door. Amara got up quickly. Who could it be? It was still early, and although Amara was an early riser, it was too early for a social call. A third knock, followed by a woman's voice. "Awake and shine." It was Rosie. Amara sat up quickly. She wondered what Rosie wanted so early in the morning.

"Do enter," said Amara.

Rosie opened the door and entered the room. She carried a basket of clothing, oils, jewelry, royal adornments, and a pleasant smile on her face.

"I pray thee rested well during the eve hours, my lady. Now we must wake up here in the palace; toils are done early before the blistering heat of the high Sun."

"Toils, slave work?" Amara asked. "I toil not for maidservants attend to my needs," Amara said. It was true. Amara did nothing in her home but tended to the garden and sometimes fed the sheep. She had maidservants to bathe and dress her.

"Surely you do not think the palace is kept without servants," laughed Rosie. "Yes, everyone offers service. The women spin carpets, cook meals, tend gardens, attend flocks, dance, play music for guests, and have royal children." Amara was perplexed. Was the role of a harem girl a glorified servant?

"This morn begins the new moon purification," Rosie informed in a melodic voice. "Purification," repeated Amara—another thing she did not understand. The damsel bathed daily, cared for her body, used oils, and kept the Mikveh rituals following menses. Was there something she was missing? "You were handpicked and chosen to stand before King Dawit for deflowering," Rosie said excitedly. Amara was shocked. She turned her face away from Rosie, for she did not want to be deflowered by King Dawit.

Rosie could see that Amara was uncomfortable. "The King has been lonely since Zenia has been banished. If it pleases him to look upon thy beauty and rejoice in his heart, you can be the Sun that shines unto his face," Rosie implored. "His spirit will not be empty, for you will be the balm that heals him." Amara wanted to cry but instead dared to ask, "What happened to Queen Zenia?"

Rosie gave her an ominous look as if Amara had said something forbidden. "She disobeyed the King and felt not his wrath," Rosie said in a different tone. "A dishonorable woman, not worthy of her husband. She should count it a blessing that she was not beheaded. Worry not about that, for it's not good for the spirit."

Outside the window, Amara heard children laughing and playing. Curious, she went to the balcony, scanning the beauty in the garden and the many children, boys and girls, in the courtyard.

The garden was beautiful with hanging plants, hyacinths, swards, shrubs, and vivid pink flowers everywhere. In the middle of the garden was a large tree whose roots spread far and wide with many fruit branches. The tree was remarkable and adorned with diamonds, emeralds, rubies, and many precious jewels. Rosie joined Amara on the balcony. "Those are the royal children. They are going hunting with the King."

"All those children belong to the King?" Amara asked, quite amused. "Yes, but none are royal," Rosie said before she caught herself. "They are not royal," Amara repeated, perplexed. "Are they not the children of the King; what makes them not royal?" The curious girl quickly changed the conversation, pointing at a large evergreen tree in the middle of the garden. "That tree, are those real rubies, diamonds, and sapphires? That's astonishing."

"It is the Cypress of Kashmar. It came from a branch the prophet Zoroaster had carried away from Paradise. It will not cause the fall of man but provide them with eternity and a long life," Rosie said proudly. Amara did not understand what Rosie was talking about. It was all strange.

"I have some fresh clothing for you," Rosie said, pulling out a pair of light flowing pants, tapered at the ankles, with soft matching boots, a midriff fitted blouse, and a cloak from the basket and gave it to Amara. "I will get a servant girl to braid your hair." Rosie exited the room, walking backward, a gesture shared by all house servants. Amara immediately started dressing while taking in her surroundings. Her room was beautiful. The playful laughter of the unroyal children could still be heard from a distance.

Breakfast in the royal dining room was no little thing. Amara arrived in a large room with a vast group of people waiting. All freshly bathed and dressed in white, the servants busied themselves preparing the table. The large table was elegantly arranged with golden plates, golden drinking goblets, and fresh-cut flowers. The food, rose water, an array of flatbreads, fruits, preserved apricots, attic figs, nasturtium leaves, cream of wheat, goat's milk, and every type of fowl eggs.

The harem girls sat by the kitchen on the far side of the large hall.

Vanessa sat beside Amara, looking for a companion because she was homesick. "Morn," she greeted Amara. "Vanessa is what I am called."

"Morn," responded Amara quietly. "Amara is my name." An older woman saw the conversation between the two maidens and started walking in their direction.

The King sat at the head of the table, and on his right side was the cupbearer, Nehemiah, who tasted everything before King Dawit ate from it. On the left side sat Gabe, the King's bodyguard. The girls in the harem were far away, hardly able to see the King. Finally, Mother Queen entered, dressed in a sheer flowing white gown, and sat at the head table with her son.

"Have you seen him, whispered Amara to Vanessa?" "The King?" asked Vanessa as she grabbed a flatbread and tore it in two with her hands.

Suddenly, there was a swat on her hand.

"Ouch," she cried out in pain and looked to see an older woman with evil eyes. She said something both girls did not understand but knew not to do. The rest of the girls, including Amara, lowered their eyes. They did not want to be next. Soon, the girls would learn there were rules, restrictions, and rituals, and refusing was not an option.

Later that morning, Queen Mother Adi sat in her majestic comfortable chair, surrounded by servant girls fanning her with large peacock feathers. It was her quiet spot. A small group of girls quietly played music on stringed instruments while others danced in light dancing clothing.

Todd, 17, entered the pleasant spot with a big smile. The girls stopped to look, for he was stunning—the governor of Susa. Mother Queen was refreshing herself with a soma drink when she saw him approaching.

"The sunshine has risen, and my heart rejoices at the presence of my nephew. It's like seeing an angel."

"Mother Queen," Todd said, kissing her hand. "My eyes see the face of a goddess," he replied, offering her a little blue box. "This is for you."

"Todd, thy spoils me, my nephew. What is this thy offer me?" she asked, reaching for the gift and gesturing for him to sit down. She loved her nephew, and he always brought her exceptional offerings. "Open it," Todd said, his grey eyes excited. He resembled her brother, a tall, bronze, handsome man who turned heads when he entered rooms.

Wasting no time, the Queen Mother unwrapped the gift. It was a beautiful gold-decorated box. When she opened it, it was playing music. "Oh my," she exclaimed like a child, "melody cometh forth from this little box."

"I made it for you, and my heart delights seeing thy face light up like the Sun," said Todd.

"I love thy clever gifts," she said, embracing the music box to her bosom like a precious gem.

Mother Queen clapped her hands, and a young girl appeared for instruction.

"Bring a refreshing drink for my guest." The Mother Queen's eyes followed her out, immediately focusing on her visitor. "Tell me, nephew, some news to delight my soul," she said with a smile. "Thy soul should delight in our success, as we have added two hundred triremes to the Persian fleet in preparation for the next campaign to Greece."

Mother Queen suddenly looked distressed, and the beauty drained from her face, making her look like an old crow. She was not in favor of a campaign to the Aegean Islands. Her late husband had returned ill from the last campaign to that strange part of the world and died shortly after. She hoped her son would abandon that idea. Todd noticed a change in her demeanor. "My lady, the Sun has left thy face. Do tell me why?" He sipped his refreshing cold pomegranate drink.

"Oh Todd, I am weary of Dawit. He thinks as a child, and his ways are not those of his fathers'. He is not a man of war. He has not borne any royal children, only children by concubines.

But should he meet the same faith as his father, there would be no heir. What would become of the throne? I would go to my grave tormented for eternity."

"May the Queen live forever," Todd rebuked. "No such fate will meet Dawit. He has an unstoppable army."

Others in the family would gladly take that role if he died, thought Todd. Adi smiled by no means a comfortable smile. On the contrary, the Mother Queen seemed genuinely concerned.

"Many conspire against my son, reporting to the barbarians, Hellenes."

"Traitors sell their souls to the enemy when conspiring against the King. The punishment for such an offense is sanctioned by the antidemonic law, a slow and torturous death," replied Todd.

Todd's intention for visiting Mother Queen was to learn about Amara. The girl he loved was being held in the harem. He wanted to redeem her as a privileged member of the Royal Family. The King offered girls from the harem to his generals and captured kings to strengthen regional and foreign diplomacy. So, he wanted to speak for Amara and pay the bride's price. "My lady," he was uneasy. "There is a damsel in the royal harem," his face reddened.

"Speak, dear Todd," the Mother Queen encouraged. She could honor him with anything his heart desired. Before Todd could say anything, Artabanus entered the room. "Queen Zenia has arrived at the courts and has requested to see King Dawit," he announced.

CHAPTER THIRTEEN

THE THRONE ROOM

The gold and silver throne faced the entrance of the Shushan Palace, where King Dawit ruled and reigned over the earth. His curly, frizzy hair was topped with a smooth crown, combed over the forehead, and fluffed to the neck. His beard was cut square at the waist with horizontal rows of curls. He was adorned with gold earrings, bracelets, and a large gold collar, all inset with jewels. King Dawit loved taking off his ornaments and showering them on his visitors. The train of his Phoenician purple robe, embroidered with gold, filled the courthouse. The robe, a gift from Queen Zenia, was designed especially for him. It was rumored to be valued at 12,000 talents.

An army of soldiers and the Royal Bodyguards surrounded the throne. Next to him were two attendants dressed in purple robes and purple shoes. Their hats were lower, and their beards were rounded, not square. One held the royal parasol with curving ribs and a pomegranate top. The other military chamberlain bore napkins and a fly flapper. Satraps also sat on a gold dais to receive their supplicants and envoys. The chiliarch, the Grand Vizier, and the Master of Ceremony introduced the petitioners and councils to the royal presence.

King Dawit held a gold scepter in his right hand and lotus flowers in his left. His feet rested on the footstool of a bull's feet. Several courtiers and eunuchs wearing bashlyks stood to his left. A Median officer with an embroidered wide fillet stood bolt upright and watched the crowds enter the court. He had a bow case, an ornamental ax, and a dagger on his belt. Before Dawit stood two Persian soldiers with cylindrical hats; they tended two small pillars with pyramidal objects on top, the sacred fire altars burning incense. On the right hand was Gabe, the King's bodyguard, dressed in a cavalry custom, twisted headband, and stooped forward in a slight bend with his only hand to his hips in greeting.

Two scribes stood by, holding a bucket of clay tablets for notetaking. Merchants from all tribes and nations, petitioners, and ordinary people lucky enough to be admitted to the courtroom jostled for space. Two men of similar social standing greeted each other with lip kissing. Other men of lower status prostrated to higher-ranking citizens. Many came to petition the King bearing gifts. Envoys, emissaries, and accused prisoners of treason sought fair justice from the heavenly-appointed monarch. The Majesty wielded a two-way sword, cutting heads in the name of justice.

The assembly was loud.

Zenia, dressed in her royal apparel, stood in the inner court of the King's house. A Magi escorted her to the south side near the front.

King Dawit raked the crowd of people with his eyes. At first, he could not distinguish people's faces because of the gloom in his heart.

After a few moments, his eyes adjusted.

Then he saw her, escorted by a Magi.

His heart skipped a beat. Zenia's head was covered, but her walk was unmistakable. Slowly, she turned, showing her soft, curvy cheek and imperious eyes. He stopped breathing. He could not tear his gaze away. His frown suddenly turned into a smile, and their eyes met. Time stood still momentarily as they remembered they were friends and lovers. The King stared straight ahead, avoiding his mother's eyes burning a hole through him. Without hesitation, he extended his golden scepter toward her.

Zenia held her gaze directly as she drew near him, prostrated, and touched the top of his scepter. There was a long silence in the hall; you could hear a pin drop.

"What wish thou, Queen Zenia, and what is thy request?" asked King Dawit. Zenia lifted her head to look at the adorned King. Her eyes searched for his soul before she spoke. "If it seems good, thy Lord, let the King come this day unto a banquet I have prepared for him." The entire assembly went silent. Mother Queen stood up, holding her hand. "Thy evil and wicked woman...perverse in heart, you shall not see my son; remove that woman from the court!"

A guard approached Zenia. Before he could lay a finger on her, the Magi decapitated him. Mother Queen screamed, horrified, as the body twitched on the ground, and the head rolled in front of the King's throne, the eyes moving around wildly from shock. What was he going to do? The court officers were stunned. The King hesitated a moment longer, then stood up, dropping the flowers from his hand. It was very silent, a tense moment.

King Dawit glanced to either side, wondering whether anyone else would lose their head. He had decreed to banish Zenia from his presence, yet he had been sickened with guilt for what he had done. These thoughts consumed his heart with fear, for the Nowruz celebration was approaching. The celebration of the King of Gods, Ahura Mazda. The godhead who legitimized him as a Monarch on earth. The empty chariot drawn by white horses was ever-present in his thoughts, for his unrighteous behavior could cost him divine grace. "Make haste, do not touch the Queen," the King heard himself say. Everyone was surprised, including the King.

He could not believe his response to the defiance of his decree. Everyone was astonished by the King's spontaneous response. Had he forgotten the law he signed? He could not remember why he made such a foolish decision, but he knew it was wrong, for nightmares haunted him. He owed Zenia an apology, and no one would interfere with that, including his mother. The King then said, "I will attend thy banquet." No one dared to oppose the King and remind him of his decree. The wise men were wise and held their wagging tongues, for their heads were dangling on a string.

"Thank you, my Lord," Zenia said sincerely. "There is a tent outside the city gates, which I have prepared for the banquet."

She bowed to the King and slowly exited, walking backward. Under the arch, she could still see the King's eyes burning for her. No one looked at Zenia. Most appeared to be half dazed, and most believed she did not do anything wrong. She left the throne room, hardly believing in her luck.

Mother Queen Adi was fuming. "You idim fool," she said with sudden viciousness as she stomped out of the courtroom like a hornet on fire. Her voice had a dangerous note. The people stood quietly in the courtroom, but the chattering of their tongues hit the roof outside the hall.

Women and children approached Queen Zenia outside the court. A woman leading a stubborn goat offered it as a gift to Zenia. Touched by her generosity, she accepted the gift. The Magi, accompanied by a senior assembly member, escorted her to the six-horse coach. The infamous Queen rode away, waving and greeting the people.

From an early age, Zenia had been a savvy investor and a powerful noble property owner in her own right. Following her marriage to Dawit, the late King Darius granted Zenia a collection of villages and estates in northwestern Syria as her fiefdom. Her Uncle Norman managed her holdings and collected from the renters. Zenia spent most of her time in Babylonia, where she spun her wealth and influence as a leader and landowner in Syria into a series of large estates around Babylon and Nippur. She was close with the Satraps of Egypt and Median, the powerful Murashu merchant family.

Zenia had a network of spies and informants that kept her abreast of what was happening at the Susa Palace. It was unsurprising to hear that Mother Queen had instigated her removal from the Queen's throne. Her mother-in-law had always been jealous of her relationship with her late husband, King Darius. He had arranged the marriage between Dawit and Zenia as a peace treaty, which the Queen Mother did not approve of.

CHAPTER FOURTEEN

WOO ME

The banquet tent was perfectly arranged to the King's liking. The room was lit with oil lamps, and the table was set with silver and gold wine vessels. The cooks worked hard to prepare the goat and an ox, a favorite of the King. The room was adorned with comfortable cushions. Floral arrangements of luscious colors filled the tent. Zenia had covered the ground with refined Persian carpets. She had brought dancing girls from Babylon, jugglers, musicians, and a King's game. Of course, everything had to be perfect. Plenty of fish, meats, wine, rice, long grain couscous, and the King's favorite dessert, rice pudding, flavored with orange blossoms and water from the Choaspes River.

King Dawit himself could not think of anything else after accepting the invitation to the banquet. His spirit was lifted with songs when Gabe entered his chambers.

"His Majesty is in joyous spirits with a new song in his heart," Gabe joked.

"I follow the eternal truths and recognize the better life. Ahura-Mazda, the wise, makes blessings lift my heart from evil deeds. A true foe of a liar I listened to, but the righteous spirit strongly supports my Queen."

"That makes my heart rejoice, Shah. I want nothing more than for you to shine like the Sun."

Zenia was extra careful as she prepared herself with salts from the Red Sea. Servants had brought in a portable bathtub of scented water.

She decided to wear a long, sheer purple gown embroidered with gold trimming, golden earrings, and a necklace, her lengthy hair in a braid. Her body was anointed in purification, for being with the God of the earth was spiritual.

At twenty-one, she was still beautiful and desirable.

The baby was also scrubbed clean. After his bath, he was wrapped in swaddling gift cloths. The baby was no longer scrawny.

He was chubby with a dimpled smile—a perfect little cherubic with pink cheeks, fine curly hair, and a divine child.

Zenia looked at the fussing babe, squirming and protesting. He did not like being wrapped like a mummy. At first, she was worried when the child opened his eyes. "His eyes," she said to the Magi, "one is azure and the other serpentine. Is he blind?"

"Thy child is not blind," the Magi assured. "He shall revolt and bore a crown of supremacy."

A caravan of people arrived with the King, the cupbearer, Gabe, the bodyguard, and royal officers.

Four men carried him on a carpet, for the King could not walk on the ground outside the palace. He wore loose white trousers, a Kandy Kolor shirt, and a tiara. He looked young and full of curiosity. Zenia wanted to appease him; her proposal was unusual, but King Dawit had the power and resources.

That evening, the King was showered with dancing girls, songs of praise, and stringed instruments. His heart lifted with laughter and joy. High in his spirit, he tossed golden bracelets to the entertainers.

The Royal couple sat on rugs cushioned with ample pillows. Both were quiet in thought but happy to be together.

A large cooking pot of vegetables and ox tails was placed on a short table before King Dawit. His mouth watered. The aroma of fresh herbs filled the room.

Gabe smiled, and his mouth was also watered. He loved oxtail stew himself, but the joy of watching the delighted King made him happy.

King Dawit offered the Baji blessings.

The guest washed their hands while the cupbearer evaluated the stew. "Let the curse be upon me if poison is found upon this food," he said and assessed. His eyes slowly closed, not because the food was poison but because of its savory taste. Dawit anxiously awaited the approval as he was ravenous. The King's smile was like seeing the moon's reflection on the Nile River as he enjoyed his meal.

The tent made of camel hair was divided into two chambers and separated by a double curtain of the finest quality. The outer chamber where the feast was held was much larger, enclosed by a curtain.

On the tables were golden lampstands with three branches on each side, affording seven lamp lights supplied with olive oil. The altar of incense was in front of the tent. The interior chamber was the sleeping quarters of the Queen and where the royal baby was being attended.

A young maiden appeared with a wine vessel and fresh grapes on vines. That night, the wine served was not fermented but fresh from the essence of the grapes. Zenia knew fermented wine made her husband see illusions. She remembered how hastily he treated her during one of his drunken fits of anger. The maiden pressed the grapes into the golden chalice for the King to drink.

After the main course, another servant brought the dessert, rice pudding. Dawit's face lit up like a child. His haggard, guilty, and grieved face morphed into a handsome man. King Dawit did not know what to think. He did not deserve this royal treatment. In his mortal mind, he had followed the path of the liar. He was both man and god, bestowed with blessings to act with discernment by the Divine Spirit and represent Righteousness on earth, but the man in him had been unrighteous. He looked at beautiful Zenia in wonder. Did she still love him?

Zenia's eyes searched his soul. What was he thinking? Did he still desire her? Must he obey a decree he signed while blinded in drunkenness?

Did God say it was wrong, or was it his advisors? Theirs was a domestic dispute that had become a farce. "What wisheth thou, Queen Zenia, and what is thy request?" King Dawit broke the silence.

"Thou wisheth to engage in the King's game," responded Zenia, smiling. Dawit did not expect that. They had shared tender moments when they played, outwitting each other, giggling when a valuable piece was taken, and outraged when losing. Dawit did not like losing. It made him agitated, especially if he lost his queen.

Zenia knew this but did not intend to capture his queen that night. The king's game was played on an ivory framed board with seventy-two silver and gold squares and sixteen pieces that represented Kings, Queens, rooks, bishops, knights, and pawns. The two chess masters studied the pieces. The Royal Guards, Gabe, and even the Magi stood around watching.

Dawit opened the game. The moves were quick and aggressive, cessations of pins, skewers, forks, and discovered attacks. The game was exhilarating as the two experts brawled, astonishing those who watched. King Dawit won, and his ego was inflated with pride. He had never beaten her before.

"I am the King, the Lord of the Lands, appointed by Ahura Mazda. The needs of the people I know about, but to attend the celebration of Marduk, conflicts with the Nowruz celebrations," he said. He thought Zenia was going to appeal for the Akitu celebration.

Secretly, he cursed his father and grandfather for allowing idol worship in the subjugated cities.

"My King, if it pleases thee, it is a desperate time for my people whom your father promised to protect.

I have come to make a proposal for my people, fearful of losing my head. Your leaders have banished me from thy presence for no fault."

"What wisheth thou, Queen Zenia, and what is thy request?" Dawit interrupted.

"I know thy King follows the laws of Asha, and I pray my King remembers my forefathers were also kings. Therefore, I petition you to make me Queen of Babylon, for Marduk provided the seed and will give the corn and wheat if I stand for the people."

"Grand request, my lovely Queen," said King Dawit. He knew Zenia to be forward.

Zenia did not wait for the answer. Instead, she said, "A gift from God, I offer thee." She clapped her hands, and a nurse stepped out behind a curtain carrying a basket. She placed the basket before the King. One of the King's advisors inspected the basket's contents. Was it a head? He wondered. He opened the basket, and inside, he saw the child. Confused, he motioned for another advisor to approach the basket; he announced, "A child."

King Dawit was beyond belief and leaped onto the ground. The guests were astonished. A cacophony of murmuring reverberated around the tent. "A gift from God," announced Zenia. Another man tried to step forward to look at the child, but Gabe whipped him away. "Dare no one approach the child," he ordered. An Elder stood before the child. He slowly started unwrapping the swaddling clothes. The babe woke up, piercing the ears of all with squeals of protest. The King looked astonished and wondered if it was a male child, the child for whom he had long waited.

"A male child," announced the Elder, clearing his throat. The unrobed child showered the room with urine. Laughter filled the room. Embarrassed, the Elder wiped his face.

"Bring the child closer so that I may inspect him," said King Dawit. He had long waited for a son but had believed Zenia to be barren. The babe was in a high throttle of anger.

His piercing cries echoed in the desert.

CHAPTER FIFTEEN

THE GARDEN

"Thy spirit of fire, bring forth the child that I may know him," ordered the King.

"Do not touch the child," said one of the advisors. "If you do, you will acknowledge him as your son, the crown Prince of the Achaemenid Empire." The other advisors in the room gestured in agreement. "This child was not born in the marriage bed, for Zenia has been banished," said one of the advisors. "My Lord, you cannot recognize this illegitimate child, he will not ascend to the throne. You will need the support of your royal council. It will be chaotic."

"Tell me, advisor of the liar, why have you attempted to misguide me," replied the King, to everyone's amazement. A new strength had arisen inside the King, a power he had lost many years prior. The Shah took the child unto his bosom. Lifting the child, he spoke, "Giver of truth, give thy truth. Giveth thy help of the Divine Spirit, appointed to me, to realize my state."

Dawit then demanded the tent be cleared of spectators and servants. He wanted a private moment with Zenia. Gabe immediately cleared the tent and stood outside the curtain. The Royal soldiers stood guard. As soon as the room was emptied, the nurse took the baby, leaving the Royal couple alone.

"Ya Hayati whom my soul loveth, the darkness of my soul sees the Sun when I look at thee," said King Dawit. His voice was husky in Zenia's ear. He took her into his arms and passionately kissed her. Zenia was surprised. "You kiss me with the kisses of thy mouth, for your love is better than wine," she replied, kissing him back. "Draw me, my King, into your chambers. Each night away from you, on my bed, I sought you, whom my soul loved. I sought you but found you not."

King Dawit stroked her hair, embracing her tenderly. "My dove, thy art in the clefts of my heart, in the secret places where I see only thy countenance and hear your sweet voice. Forgive me, for I have sinned against you with foolishness." Queen Zenia's eyes filled with tears. Dawit held her for a long time as they wept.

"Come, my beloved, drink from my breast, for I have compared you to a company of horses in Pharaoh's chariots."

Dawit smiled. His Queen had always been forward. "Your breasts are like two young roes that are twins, which feed among the lilies," he said, removing her gown. Then, tenderly, he led her to the cushions, covering her body with kisses.

"Until the daybreak and the shadows flee, I will climax with my spouse and ravish his heart within my garden," Zenia moaned in ecstasy.

"Your lips are like honey, and milk is under my tongue, and the smell of your garment is likened to the smell of lavender. Thy cheeks are comely with rows of jewels, your neck with chains of gold. O thou art fairest among women, my love lavishes in thy garden."

"Come, my beloved, lie all night between my breasts," Zenia encouraged.

"Behold, thou art beautiful, my beloved, pleasant also our bed is green." He removed his royal garments, scattering them on the floor, and joined her on the pillows.

The flickering of the lamplights illuminated as he gently moved on top of her and passionately kissed.

She responded with love nibbles on his neck, sending chills up his back. Zenia stroked his long, thick, curly hair, scented with musk. His massive body enveloped her small frame.

"Oh yes, lavish me. I looked for you and could not find you by night," he whispered huskily in her ears. "O' fairest among women."

Gabe's face became beet red when he heard sensuous sounds outside the curtain, and he smiled as the King roared like a lion.

Mother Queen's anger had not subsided. She remembered what Zenia had done and how she had circumvented the decree. Adi prowled around the palace like a lioness that had not been fed for days. Anyone the Queen Mother met in the corridors, even the most trustworthy, feared for their lives, afraid of being thrown into prison, tortured, or executed on a whim. Her attendants, including Rosie, tip-toed around her, trying not to catch her evil eye. The courtiers wrung their hands in frustration as the majestic woman recoiled as if in pain. She felt like a dog kicked out of the way, curled in her bed sulking. Her honor was being defaced by Zenia, and Mother Queen would not have it. The thoughts infuriated her, and she longed to kill someone, anyone.

Rosie called for the Royal Doctor. It was unhealthy for her when she got that way, wallowing in self-pity and putting stress on her heart. Rosie was very worried. She tried giving Mother Queen a strong tea. Which she angrily threw against the wall. Rosie ran out before the offense was directed at her.

Dr. Democedes, a Greek with sage hair, arrived. "Thy Mother Queen's path of thoughts has gone vile," said Rosie. "She needs something to calm her down." This was not the first time Mother Queen had this type of episode. Dr. Democedes knew how to calm her. Entering the room, he saw her crying on the bed. He felt compassion for her. There were times when she needed someone to talk to and times when a tender touch would calm her down. He would figure it out.

"My Lady," said the Doctor. Adi sat on her bed, always glad to see Dr. Democedes. He was a gentleman with tender hands. Her face was swollen from crying. "My Queen," he said lovingly. "What is ailing the pearl of my heart, causing anguish?" His smile lit up the room. She was very special to him; he had healed her from a lump on her breast. "What would help my lady, a sedative tea or a gentle touch?" he asked.

Adi smiled; she loved it when he gave her choices, empowering her. "A little tender touch," she whispered shamelessly, disrobing. The excellent Doctor performed magic with his tender hands, easing her mind and calming her spirit. She suddenly remembered Zenia and started weeping again. "Zenia beguiled him with trickery," she cried. "What is this bastard child she brings?"

His eyes filled with compassion for the royal lady. "My lady, excite not thy heart," advised Dr. Democedes, removing his robe.

CHAPTER SIXTEEN

WHO TO DEVOUR

"Have you heard the news of the morn?" asked Artabanus as he entered the Garden. Mother Queen Adi was still sore from the night before and in a repulsive mood. King Dawit was accountable only to Mazda Ahura. Humans, beasts from the air, water, and earth, answered him. Mother Queen's waning spirit had a rough time accepting this reality. Since he was a child, she had tried to manipulate and control him, but that spell was quickly fading.

"My Lady is not chirpy this morn," Artabanus said. "I am sensing a waxing of spirit."

"O ye mindful to learn," said Adi, in a grumpy mood. Artabanus wondered if it would be wise to break the news when she was in such a foul mood.

"Tell me, O Artabanus, the morn news," she replied.

"Thy son, King Dawit, has bestowed blessings that all may know of his power." Adi sat up straight to listen more attentively. She wanted to hear everything. "That's not all the King has done," he continued, pacing back and forth.

"What new burdens hath my son added to the toils of my heavy-laden spirit," she said, standing up from her royal throne. The soma cocktail was starting to take effect. The girls, fanning her with ostrich feathers, scattered as soon as she stood up.

"Your son bestowed renewed power and authority to Zenia thence appointed her as Queen of Babylon." Artabanus magnetic eyes were penetrating Adi for a response. Adi could hardly believe what she had heard as she paced back and forth like a caged lioness. "My son does not know the external truths and does not recognize the better life." Her voice echoed throughout the garden, reaching the ears of the harem girls in the adjacent garden preparing their dance for the Nowruz celebrations.

Artabanus had to be delicate with his sister, acting with discernment. The impetuous woman was capable of torture. "My son, bestowed by the spirit and fire, knows not the truth, nor shares the Divine spirit appointed, for the better portion to know. Therefore, I should purge the dynasty of Zenia's daevas. Now, you listen to me, my dear brother." Her eyes narrowed. "There dwells in the desert of Arabia a man named Ahmed Abdul, East of Elam and West of the desert by Arabia. Go and hire him as an emissary to destroy the daevas of Babylon and sever the head of the snake."

"Mother Queen," replied Artabanus, uninterested; "Hiring emissaries requires the King's approval."

"I AM THE KING!" she shouted. "Do as I say, for the eternal truths, and recognize the better life." Artabanus was ambitious and desired to become ruler of Greece, but that act could cost him his life if King Dawit learned of the plot.

The Battle of Marathon had been an embarrassment and a humiliation to the Persian Empire. Artabanus will not stop until Persia is avenged. Day and night, he taunted the King, saying, 'The Greeks humiliated your father; it's been eight years, and no vengeance has been made for him.' That morning, he and King Dawit had a conversation. "It has been eight years; the military is a thousandfold, the navy two hundredfold, and the footbridge completed. The Aegean Islands calls for the

King to rule and reign." The King looked at him and said, "After the Nowruz celebrations, I, King Dawit, will campaign and command both land and sea in the Aegean." That was exciting news for Artabanus. Finally, King Dawit was ready to campaign against the foes of the Achaemenid Empire. A long-awaited strength and courage hath risen in the King that had been latent for eight years. He was unsure if he wanted to share this with Mother Queen Adi. She was full of rage, acting like a mad woman. "Adi, I am not sure emissaries to Babylon is a wise move," his hypnotic eyes narrowed. "That might stir a rebellion and usurp military resources that could serve best for the Spring campaigns."

"You dare deny my request!" she shouted. The damsels in the garden could hear her and feared for Artabanus.

"Yes," said Artabanus firmly, "Only the King can mobilize emissaries. Persia rules Babylon, King Dawit has appointed Zenia as Queen, and there is peace. Tis not wise to stir up a storm."

After a minute of contemplation, Mother Queen Adi faked a smile and changed her tune. "I have been robbed of human compassion. I must practice being astute and be pleased with the help of the Divine Spirits appointed to me...come," she motioned with her hands. "Sit and refresh thyself with rose water." A servant girl entered the Garden with a vessel of ice-cold drink. Mother Queen drank to quench the fire burning inside. It was going to be a long, dry, humid, busy day.

Amara was sitting in the garden when she thought she heard Mother Queen Adi shouting at someone and wondered what would happen if she packed her things and left the palace. Was she a prisoner? Why couldn't she go home to be with Aunt Martha? Her uncle Kaleb had not been heard from since she arrived at the palace.

The Ethiopian Vanessa entered the Garden with a vessel full of flavored ice. She sat on the edge of the pool next to Amara. They shared a quiet moment, enjoying their treats. All morning, the girls had labored, weeded, trimmed, and edged the massive Garden. It was the most work they had ever done, and the girls were exhausted. Living in the harem was not fun. One had to rise before the morning star to do the chores. There was always competition among the girls: who could dance better, sing better, and who was next to the King's chamber? The shining stars, the best of the best, would go before the King. The rest were spares used for entertainment.

Sometimes, the King would visit the Zenana when they were at work or play. If there was one that had been purified and he so desired, he would drop a silk cloth next to the girl. It was an honor in the harem, for that evening, the King would deflower that maiden.

It was crucial that the multicultural girls supported each other and developed strong relationships in the hostile environment. Mother Queen Adi paid careful attention. She liked to pin one girl against the other and then punish both. They had to live in harmony; fighting, gossiping, and sabotaging one another was frowned upon and severely punished. These behaviors were considered to be influenced by daevas.

"I have a fable for you," Vanessa said, laughing, her large dark brown eyes shimmering. Amara looked around to ensure no one was listening, especially Rosie, who was always snooping around, dropping her ears. "Do tell, has the King turned into a toad?" giggled Amara. "Yes, and we do not have to kiss him," laughed Vanessa. The girls giggled. "Giggle not, for this is a house of mourning," Amara said, trying to be serious. "Do tell me the tale so that I won't weep."

"There was once a beautiful girl who wandered into the deep jungle," started Vanessa in her storytelling voice. "Not having anything to eat all day, she was hungry. She found some berries and went to wash them in a nearby pond, not knowing there lived a magical toad in the pond. The big green toad wore a golden crown and a purple robe. 'Who is tramping on my pound?' Croaked the toad, his large green eyes glowing. "Oh, a talking toad," exclaimed the young girl. I am the king of this pond whilst you have made impure, washing berries in it.' "O, please pardon me, Your Highness," said the young girl and started to leave. Before she could get far, the toad was upon her and locked her in a small room under the pond. There, she stayed for many days. The longer she stayed, the sadder she became. The King toad did not want her to be sad. He did not want her to die ill. He longed to make her his queen.

Vanessa surveyed the area to make sure they were alone and continued. "The girl was sad and heartbroken. Every time the toad visited her, she cried and cried. This worried the toad. One day, the toad offered her half of his kingdom if she only smiled once."

'Half of his kingdom?' laughed Amara. "Yes, but the girl asked that he give her a harp, for she had the power to turn the harp into a magical instrument." Two other girls ran into their quiet spot, chasing each other, laughing, and playing around.

"The King toad presented the beautiful girl with a beautiful harp of gold and silver. She played a lovely melody that caused the toad to fall into a deep sleep. While he slept, the girl escaped and was never heard of again," Vanessa concluded. 'I wish I had a magical harp,' said Amara, her blue eyes dreamy.

"Are you going to Persepolis?" asked Vanessa. "Were you chosen to attend the Nowruz celebrations?"

"Nay, Rosie said I must complete the next purification phase. She waits for salt from the Nile River and Cypress bark from the Pacific for the next ritual," said Amara.

"The secrets of these treatments, dare you speak of?" Vanessa laughed; "Why does it take a year to cleanse one banbishnan?" Amara smiled, her blue eyes sparkling. "I do not understand either. Twelve lunar months of baths, soaks, massages, purging, priming, pruning, and pumping for the peach bareness of one night with the King," she looked distressed. "Some damsels return weeping, with blood issues that must be mended," she whispered to Vanessa. Vanessa gasps, putting her hand on her mouth. "Pray the oils and rituals prepare thy temple for the torture," Vanessa replied, her eyes wide with fear.

"A brute force, I am not inflamed with enthusiasm," Amara said, looking around. "Perhaps I can be pardoned. But in haste, I've done no wrong, for I have no desire for punishment."

"Delight in pain is man's cruelty in the fringes of brokenness. So, I pray for deliverance and shriveled phallic," Vanessa comforted.

"There comes Rosie," alerted Amara. Rosie smiled at the girls. "I have been seeking for you, Vanessa. You shall accompany the King and his guest for the Nowruz celebration. I have prepared a chest with your belongings. The caravan leaves in the morn."

"Vanessa is thy hand servant; why not choose another damsel," contested Amara. "There are other hand servants for your choice. Pick another. Vanessa will not be denied," answered Rosie in a crude tone.

Vanessa greatly feared. Two nights prior, a herculean shadow had appeared in the hall. It was a spine-chilling, scary frame of a giant with a long, square beard. Vanessa ran and hid in her room. Later, she learned the King roamed throughout the palace, seeking out what was open and what was hidden and wrong so he could make right.

CHAPTER SEVENTEEN

THE ARABS

Mother Queen Adi stood before a pond, gazing at her reflection with a gruesome smile. "A shower of locusts from the deep desert for you, my beloved Queen Zenia; let's see who will deliver you now," she laughed. Rosie saw the Mother Queen laughing. She could not hear what was said, but at least Adi was in a good mood. The young servant girl holding the parasol for Mother Queen heard. It was dark thoughts that scared her. Mother Queen was unstable like ocean waves, given to swells of fits. Previously, one of the servant girls was whipped to death for breaking a flask of oil. Another girl was mutilated, her ears, nose, and lips cut for trying to run away.

That day, Mother Queen went on a long trip. "If anyone inquires of me, say I have taken up to my chambers for purification," she told Rosie.

Ahmed Abdul was an Arab with a large, crooked nose, ice-cold black eyes, and void of cleanness. Suspiciously, he welcomed the caravan to the camp. He was the Jarraray of his tribe, commanding more than 1,000 soldiers. Arabs were different from all of the other races. They lived in the naked desert under the indifferent heaven, distrusting everyone. By day, they were fermented by the hot sun and dizzied by the beating winds. At night, they were stained by the dew and shamed into pettiness by the innumerable minutes of the silence of stars. They were nomads of wars and raids. Looting was their primary source of sustenance. Bloodlust or revenge was always on their hands. Wounding, killing, or ephemeral pains were their way of life. They lived by truth and untruth, belief and unbelief. There were no shades, only black and white. Welding the sword, disemboweling, torturing, or disfiguring their victims was the only art they knew.

A camel driver, wearing a turban and a Jubba, entered the camp leading the caravan. They stopped in front of a dusty, dirty tent. Ahmed approached the strange visitors. "My friends, how may I serve thee?"

The smell of dromedaries was unbearable. Inside the coach was a woman dressed in widow's clothing, with her face covered. Nasty black flies swamped around the coach, looking for fresh skin from which to draw blood. Large Tarantulas ran across the hot, dry desert sand. The ground was full of scorpions and desert snakes.

"Is there a cooler place to talk," asked the Turbaned driver. Ahmed belly laughed, his stomach quivering like a liver. "Oh, my friend, a desert dweller, you are not. You Satrapies live a slothful life in nobility while the rest of the world carries the burden." He gestured with his hands, "Come, I have a tent for a meeting. May I offer you a Raki?" A fetid odor followed him. The camp was desolate, void of any oases for refuge. How can people delight in such cruelty in a dry, dusty, smelly, hot environment? The driver assisted the woman out of the coach. The repulsive smell assaulted the woman's nose behind her veil, causing her to gag.

"My friend," humored Ahmed, "the desert air is too strong for ye?" Heat bugs swamped the visitors. A black tunic shielded the woman's delicate skin from the thirsty bugs. "Now, my friend, I am of slow learning; explain what the pleasure of this visit is.

"I am looking for emissaries for a secret assignment," said the woman. "Please, please have a seat," offered

Ahmed. He clapped his hands, and a shepherdess appeared. "Bring drinks for the guests. Please continue," said Ahmed, showing a mouth full of decay and rot.

"Ask no questions," the woman said. Ahmed did not particularly like negotiating with women. It was apparent that this was no ordinary woman. Who was she, he wondered. "What secret assignment doth ye speak of, and how will it benefit my people?"

"The assignment is to burn Babylon," said the unpleasant woman. "My friend, the beautiful city of Babylon belongs to King Dawit. It is surrounded by rivers and fertile land, and they are allies to my people who provide in times of famine.

"There is a price of 500 darics, 95.83% gold coins minted as booty for the task." Ahmed spits out the warm drink, clearing his voice. "No, my friend, that is too much gold, a necessity, as you can see. Look around; the surroundings are cruel, but we keep our heads, huh." Ahmed had every reason to be cautious. His entire tribe would be destined for destruction and annihilation if discovered, captured, and tried in the courts of King Dawit. But there was one principal Ahmed could fall back on in his defense: One who does not kill is killed, and one who does not fight is fought. Still, burning Babylon came with ramifications. Ahmed knew that fact better than anyone. "I know not thy strange request, my friend," continued Ahmed.

"You are being paid to burn down that city of sin," not ask questions. "Accept the work, or hold thy peace." The woman in black stood up.

"Babylon is not an easy city to assault." Ahmed's voice was seldom. "Please provide me with weapons."

"The gold will be sufficient to cover all expenses. You can use offensive weapons within your reach," replied the woman.

"My friend, a need exists for a catapult to assault the thick walls," stated Ahmed, gesturing with his hands. "Have I spoken in riddles," said the woman. "No weapons will be provided." The King's insignia marked all the weapons in the empire, and they were all accounted for. The woman would not chance the weapons being found and her plot discovered. Ahmed sensed something sinister in her voice.

The amount of gold blinded his senses, and he agreed to attack Babylon. He knew he would have to bring the Babylonians out from behind the fortified walls or use a ruse, for powering through would be impossible. "I will begin plans for the attack," Ahmed said. "One of my commanders will draw the battle plans. I will allot commanders for each section, define the assignments, identify the goal, and arm the forces." The responsibility for these tasks rested on Ahmed's shoulders because of his superiority over the others. In the end, he would bear the burden.

"The Queen and the child from Babylon are to be executed and their heads delivered to King Dawit, do you understand?" affirmed the widow. "No, I do not understand. What you ask is an awkward thing. You ask for the head of Queen Zenia and her child. More gold will be needed; this is the most difficult thing."

"Once you complete the task, more gold will be considered," answered the woman angrily.

"Mobilization of forces and recruitment of the tribe requires rations to be issued through a signed agreement," reminded Ahmed, having second thoughts.

"Are you literate?" asked the widow. Ahmed was not. He had no understanding of language, but he pretended he did. The woman sized Ahmed to be a fallen barbarian. She took a scroll from her travel bag and handed it to him. "Here is the agreement." The Arabic was unsure what he looked at, but it looked official enough.

CHAPTER EIGHTEEN

THE AKITU CELEBRATION

F rom the pathless sea, an army of men on horses, wearing turbans, gathered at the riverbank. Their mission was to burn down Babylon and capture the Queen.

In Babylon, it was the first day of the Akitu Celebrations. People traveled from various cities to evoke pity from Marduk and gain divine blessings. It was a time of repentance, psalms, lamentation for private illnesses and misfortunes, the rebirth of nature, the re-establishment of kingship by divine authority, and community gatherings. People came to seek forgiveness and security for the uncertain future and the year's harvest.

It was Spring. The dazed goddess from the city went out, wailing. The gods arrived by barge at Babylon. Nabu, took up residence in the chapel in the temple of Marduk. Gods from Nippur, Uruk, Cutha, and Kish converged on the city.

Amid all the commotion, Zenia felt rumbling on the ground, not like a sandstorm, but like horses approaching. Most people traveling for the Akitu celebration would be in caravans, with their goods to sell, livestock for sacrifices, and offerings. Their travel vibrations would not feel like approaching war horses.

Gaia had also heard the loud pounding of hooves. In the past months, there had been one devastation after another: sandstorms, beetles, flooding rivers, locusts, heat waves, and suffocating air. Gaia looked forward to a brighter future.

Everyone from Babylon and Mesopotamia, the Awilu (upper class), the Muskena (middle class), the Wardu (lower class), and especially the High Priest and the Queen, were in attendance. The courtyards were packed. It was still early morning, and already it was scorching hot. Gaia led the opening of the procession, followed by Priests and Priestesses in a somber movement of mourners.

Wails of repentance reverberated with sorrowful mourning. The future was still being determined.

Mourners parade to the sound of a sad tempo as they walk down the street dressed in sackcloth. An old man played a lamenting tune on a wind instrument. The gods were paraded on barges. Among them was the golden statue of Marduk, the creator God, son of Enki, the god of wisdom. He was the patron deity of Babylon, who had defeated Tiamat, the water serpent.

Multitudes of people filled the taverns and the inns to capacity. The sounds of goats, cattle, horses, camels, birds, and wild animals permeated the morning stillness. Initially built for rapid communication, the Royal Road was congested with commerce. The road split into two routes, one from Ecbatana along the Silk Road, the other through Susa, and southeast to Persepolis in the Zagros Mountain. Both routes were congested with tradespeople, merchants, exotic animals, and travelers attending Akitu in Babylon or Nowruz in Persepolis. Among the travelers were those who delighted in pain and cruelty, covertly concealed.

Gaia was a tall older man with an ascetic, crafty look and a long white beard. He walked painfully with a staff. Dressed in an adorned tunic with gold stars, he led the crowds to the front of the Ésagila Temple. The public gathered in the sweet, spicy, perfumed morning air. Two priests stood on both sides of Gaia, with two large Peacock fans. Gaia lifted his hands to the sky and quieted the people. "The Secret of Ésagila," he announced. It was a sad intercessory prayer. "Lord, without peer in thy wrath. Lord gracious King, Lord of the lands."

The morning star started to peek through the Eastern sky. Pillars of pale golden lights from the heavens began to align with a beam of light from the temple of Shamash in the middle of the city. The people watched in awe as reflections of light filled the temple. The Gate of Heaven opened, illuminating the heavens and earth. Thousands of people experienced mirages of celestial beings and fell on bent knees in reverence. All was quiet, if not for the sounds of animals and heat bugs in the distance and the occasional howls of wild dogs.

"Lord, who made salvation for the great gods," continued Gaia. "Lord who throweth down the strong by his glance." Gaia's face glistened with drops of sweat. Wails of lamentations from the people began to erupt like waves of blowing dry sand, reaching a peak and dying out again. Then, after a long silence, another wave peaked and diminished again. "Lord of Kings, the light of men, who dost apportion destinies, O Lord, Babylon is thy seat, Borsippa thy crown." Two men, Bel-Shimanni and Shasmash-Ariba, joined Gaia. They had been appointed to represent the people before Marduk. Later in the ceremony, they would stand before the High Priest to be slapped around for the sins committed by the Monarch.

Beltan, a high priestess dedicated to the Temple of Shamash, started feeling faint. "The heat bakes me to the ground," she whispered to Dani. She kept a close watch on Queen Zenia, who was among them.

"The vast heavens are thy body; within thine arms, thou take the strong. Within thy glance, thou grantest them grace, makes them see the light, so they proclaim thy power." Gaia's gown was drenched in sweat. Dry spittle collected on the side of his mouth, foaming like a rabid dog. He motioned for a drink.

Nabu was a tall Sumerian with no hair. He was the commander of Babylon's small army and heard the rumbling of the horses. He left the worship assembly with several soldiers and headed toward the city's gate. The people began to sense a shift of tension in the atmosphere. They could hear and feel the pounding of horses. Gaia sensed something was going on as the people's wails turned to anxious cries. He waved his hands for the people to calm down. Then, he continued with his reading. Still trying to figure out what was happening, Nabu ordered the city gates secured. Then, he sent several scribes to investigate.

Queen Zenia was ushered inside the ziggurat by Beltan. The entourage of servants followed. "My Lady, it is much too hot; let's find shade in the temple, my tongue is consumed with thirst."

King Dawit was in Persepolis, celebrating the Nowruz holidays. An usher led three grooms on tiny Nesaean Stallions. Their only harness was a headstall of round and flat beads with a small bell. A third usher preceded two empty chariots—one for the invisible Ahura Mazda and the other for the King. The sacred white horses were adorned with a headstall and a gold bit. Their bridles were covered with embroidered housing, and the reigns were comb-like metal disks with a band around the chest and another ornament by a tassel behind the forelegs. Their forelock was tufted as a lotus blossom, and the hair along the neck was trimmed to a crest.

Chariot poles were set directly into an axle, held to the wheel by a pin in the form of a nude dwarf. Twelve spokes swell in the middle. The tires were studded with considerable spikes to afford a tighter hold on the ground. At the rear, a thong assisted the upward climb of the Monarch, and a metal hand grip permitted a firmer stance for the body to be placed directly over the axle.

Champion Lions paraded around the edge on which was a royal quiver. In a separate cage, among the lions, was a tigress, Amber, Queen Zenia's beloved pet.

Courtiers, alternately Medians and Persians, completed the rows as they strode forward, fully conscious of their high dignity, dressed in robes of scarlet, crimson, purple, and gold earrings. On their hands, only a lotus flower. The appropriate gift for the spring festivals.

Representatives from different subjects marched along to present their annual gifts to the King. Each group was introduced by an usher, who, with his right hand, held the knobbed staff. With his left, he firmly grasped the hand of the leaders of the delegation. Each delegation wore its national dress and brought its most renowned products, textiles, metalwork, vases, and animals. The largest and most perfect horses from Armenia, camels from Arabia, giraffes from Africa, antelopes, horned bulls, Baboons and ostriches.

King Dawit wore an upright tiara of blue, spotted with white, and a robe worn over a white spots' chiton. The King sat under a canopy inlaid with jewels, supported by golden pillars, a rosette border, and divine symbols. His throne rested on turning silver balls.

Mother Queen Adi did not attend the ceremonies. However, she sent harem girls for the ceremony and a chosen animal for the games. Vanessa was one of the girls that was recruited for the task. The trip through the mountains on a caravan was rough and made her motion sick. She slept throughout the journey. The head harem keeper with the evil eye was responsible for the girls.

Early that morn the girls were woken up and assigned to different details. Vanessa had never seen so much riches in one location. She was given to help prepare the room for the Bazin. The Zofi, the High Priest of Ahura Mazda, was kind and patient. He instructed the girls to spread the sofreh, white linen in the room's center. Chairs were arranged around the placement. Vanessa set the table. Evil eyes watched her from a distance as The Zofi instructed her. "Two rolls of flowers, four each, go to the head cook. Get a metal tray, wine, milk, water, flowers, and fruits." Vanessa immediately left the room, happy to escape evil eyes. The other girls arranged the seven fire holders, the fire urn, and incense for the fire. Everyone was busy with the preparations. From a distance, Vanessa watched intently as Zofi prepared the Haoma. She had heard it was a drink from the gods, which would make one strong and wise. The Priest used consecrated water, sprigs of ephedra twigs, and cow's milk for the parahom liquid. After he was done, he put the infusion under the table. She was tempted with a desire to drink the nectar from the gods. The rest of the morning, she watched for an opportunity to taste the forbidden drink. The room had finally been prepared, and the girls had left to complete another task. Vanessa lingered behind. She looked to the left and the right. No one was around. She just wanted a taste. The elixir looked and smelled so good.

CHAPTER NINETEEN

GAIA

N ow, it came to pass that the gods were stored in the temples for protection. The threats to the city had disrupted the Akitu celebrations. The forty-foot statue of Marduk was back in his dwelling place, the Ésagila Temple. The idol, made of mesu wood and covered with gold, had eyes but could not see and ears but could not hear. Yet the people of Babylon considered him a friend. Gaia, was responsible for protecting the idol, making sure no one stole him. In Mesopotamia, there were many golden idols. When cities were captured, the conquering state would steal the idols from the temples to weaken the people. This caused much confusion and hardship, for the people believed the god had left them because the spirit of the god dwelled within the idol. In the past, Sennacherib had abducted Marduk, and King Nebuchadnezzar had to rescue him from the Elamites and bring him back to Babylon.

Gaia stood before the statue of Marduk, his heart pierced by the arrows of fear. He could do nothing to influence the outcomes of the situation he wanted. The High Priest tried to quiet his spirit and be fatalistic. If Marduk wanted Babylon to be safe, he would intervene on behalf of the people.

"If I ask thee for wheat, will thou send locusts to destroy?" asked Gaia. The serious-looking Marduk looked nonchalant. Flickering of the oil lamps cast large shadows on the walls. Gaia looked around, sensing a harmful spirit.

"O, Spirit of heaven, O, spirit of the earth, remember!" Gaia cried out. The gusting winds started picking up outside and blew out the lamps, sending thin wisps of smoke.

The city, usually busy with excitement, was under lockdown. Traders and peddlers pushed their loaded donkeys, camels, and horses, searching for open space to store their goods and values. Women with children carried baskets on their backs, while men led animals on chains. The men who daily gathered in the plaza gambling and throwing dice were dressed in battle gear. A line of prisoners was led across the street guarded by soldiers. They could decide to serve in the battle or lose their heads. The executioner, a stout fellow, carried a long sword and was followed by an assistant executioner, who carried the bowl to collect the heads. "Pledge ye allegiance to the service of the Queen of Babylon, ya or nay? Asked the executioner as the prison was led in front of him. If the prisoner agreed to serve the Queen in a state of emergency faithfully, they would be taken to the temple and dressed for battle. Those who disagreed bowed their head over the bowl.

The sounds of running horses and chariot wheels punctuated the air. Babylon was a fortified city. Decades before, a large ditch had been dug out outside the city's wall for protection. The walls were high and thick, studded with numerous towers and bastions to allow defensive fire in several directions. Behind the city walls that reached the heavens like mountains, the people were disturbed and hastened in the streets; they sought Marduk, saying, "Where is he held captive? This is devastating." Some wept bitterly. They repented their evil deeds a while ago, but what else can they do?

The frustration was agonizing. Mobs of fleeing people, girls screaming, mothers carrying squalling children in their arms, and aging people poured through the great processional Ishtar Gate, looking for an escape route. Some left their merchandise and possessions behind. The city was being evacuated, but some refused, for great would be their loss; instead, they preferred to stand by the Queen to protect the city, for many people had traveled to the city's outskirts for the Akitu Celebration.

At first, Zenia thought King Dawit had changed his mind and was en route to the Spring Celebrations, but the soldiers were not from the royal army. She did not know these were bloodthirsty desert pirates. Men void of morals, living and dying for the moment, with fallow minds, void of intellect, in spirit and body. Death was an honor, and suicide was impossible for these ruthless men.

"Attack the city's strongholds," said Ahmed Abdul. "In the chaos, there are opportunities we will cause mass confusion if we go into their strongholds. Burn the city's strongholds," Ahmed was filled with tremendous enthusiasm. Fear and excitement made him light-headed. He smiled nonchalantly at the horror he would bring to the city.

A scribe concealed in an underground tunnel heard what Ahmed Abdul was instructing his troops to do. He started running back up the nave, dusty and bleeding. He had a message for the Queen.

Queen Zenia recognized him from the scribe school; he had been sent to spy and bring back a report. "The enemy has crossed the river," he announced to the Queen, prostrating before her in reverence.

"What report has ye?" asked the Queen. "They come to create confusion and destroy the strongholds, I heard the leader say," the boy replied.

Nabu looked struck down for an instant but recovered his composure swiftly. "No matter!" He said, "Our foes, we will meet them all soon!"

The Magi, Gaspar, entered with a parchment in his hands. His dark eyes were hard and cold. A long time ago, his tribe and people had been almost genocide. Nevertheless, some had survived and committed themselves to servanthood to the Royal family. Queen Zenia had appointed him as a personal Armor Bearer and advisor.

"The Sun disappears. Like a swarm of plague flies, they will befall the land. The spirit of the winds disturbs the lilies with torment for the wicked approach from the deep abyss. Law and kindness they know not. Prayer and supplication, hear they not. They are hostile thorns and tussles from the deep desert," said the Magi.

Angry clouds rolled across the heavens, and their voices were heard as the storms approached. A gust of wind blew the temple door open, extinguishing the oil lamps. In the dark, Queen Zenia and Nabu exchanged looks. They had been waiting for confirmation. The city was strictly shut up; none went out or came in. Gaia called the priests and said, "Bear arms and escort the citizens outside the city."

The priests immediately led the citizens carefully to the four-city ziggurats', down long, narrow spiral staircases to level seven, where the under pathway would deposit them outside the city by the Euphrates River. Ships would sail them toward the Phoenicians. A group of women, with their faces covered, riding fighting horses, approached Queen Zenia. These women were led by Lydia, a cavalrywoman, to reinforce the garrison of Babylon. They were the temple prostitutes who had been abandoned in Babylon by their Hebrew husbands.

"We will fight with the Queen and protect the city," said Lydia. The women were known as skilled horsemen great in battle, discipline, organization, and tactical proficiencies.

CHAPTER TWENTY

BATTLE OF BABYLON

Babylon was in a state of readiness, and the city was secured. Mother Queen thought it was a small thing for the people from Babylon to be assaulted during their Spring celebrations. The Royal Military was in Persepolis with King Dawit, and Babylon only had a small army to defend their city. However, war was not alien to them. They were a well-organized society with written laws and bureaucratic strength. The city had always been more vulnerable to conquest and invasion, and it was fortified with two impenetrable walls along a water-filled moat. The thick walls were guarded by four-horse chariots that could turn around on top of them and not touch either side at three hundred feet.

General Nabu sent spies to check on the approaching swarm of soldiers. Who were they, what did they want, and who sent them? Information brought back by the spies was concerning. Arabic soldiers, ruthless, heartless killers who dismembered their victims.

"It's come to this," said Gaia, the High Priest, his face full of indignation. Never in his wildest dreams would he have thought this could happen. He suspected King Dawit was behind it, for he had a hard time believing when Queen Zenia was given rulership of Babylon. The city was a central hub of commerce and capital for King Dawit.

"Our strength comes from wisdom, to know how to disable the enemy," said Zenia. She knew the secrets of the great pyramids, designed by her grandfather for such a time as this. They were underground passages connecting to other cities to evacuate its vulnerable citizens. But there was little time to waste. She assembled peasants and temple workers to collect weapons from the people: javelins, arrows, spears, swords, and tahtib sticks. Helmets, cuirasses, and uniforms were already in stock in the temple. The women and children were evacuated first. Men and women volunteered to fight the foes who came to destroy their cities.

Zenia wondered about the attack and where it came from. She was sure it was not King Dawit who had sent them, but one could never be so sure. Like locusts on horses with long spears, they approached and needed to be slowed down. A weapon of mass destruction was what she needed. Something that would cause immediate death. There was such a person who could help her, Tapputi-Belatekaliim, the perfumer. She was a master in using rotting vipers to make a deadly poison that would kill on impact as soon as the arrows penetrated the skin. The old lady was immediately recruited to work. The arrowheads and swords were smeared with the deadly poison. Zenia wanted to bombard the enemy with arrows before they reached the city walls.

The tempestuous weather was also taking a turn. The sky was beginning to blacken.

Zenia remembered what the Magi had said, "They are hostile thorns and tussles from the deep desert, but mighty is the hand of Queen Zenia, and she will defeat the foe."

Angry clouds continued to roll across the heavens, and the voices of approaching storms could be heard from afar. Queen Zenia could feel the wind blowing against the temple doors. In the dark, she knew what she had to do. Gaia called the priests and said, "Bear seven double horns."

When the horns were blown, the armed men followed after the priests. The Queen and Nabu mounted their horses and rode down the city. Soldiers mounted and fell behind them. The procession of men at arms joined them. Their numbers were augmented with women ready with arms, and the number of men was significant. Helmets were joined to helmets, spear to spear, and elephants without numbers went with them. They marched; their hearts filled with rage. This was when man began to feel scared and looked for a chance to slip away, but their dignified pace and ceremonial atmosphere, with the townspeople supporting them, meant it would be difficult for the fainthearted to escape.

Archers took their positions in the city walls; they would always be uphill no matter how the enemy approached. At first, the Arabic army appeared stationary, but when Zenia looked again after a while, they were closer, and she could discern their motion if she concentrated. She wondered how strong they were. Two scribes came up the slope, riding fast. They spotted the Queen and went straight to her. Nabu crowded closer to hear their report.

"The enemy is approaching fast," said one of the scribes. There was a long pause. A gust of rising winds cast gloom over the city.

An expression of fear came over Queen Zenia's face. Her only choices were to kill or be killed, fight or be taken captive. What would happen to Iskander, the royal prince, if she died in the battle? She thought Norman would indeed care for him; he loved the babe and was like an Abba to him. Zenia held the baby tight before she sent him out of the city with Naomi and his caregivers.

"What is their disposition?" asked Zenia, noticing the change in the atmosphere. The sky was red and black with earth and air. Lightning danced across the sky. The Magi, not sure, thought a baleful storm was approaching the land. That morning, he had seen a comet with two tails, a sign of good fortune, but who could tear the veil from the mysterious future?

"The troops form from the middle; they are on horses armed with swords," said the other scribe. "Two hundredfold from the left, augmented with a Dust Devil's tribe. The leader is Ahmed Abdul, but he is not among them." Nabu wondered how the scribes knew this. They must have gone right into their camp and listened. That takes bravery. But where was Ahmed Abdul?

The Arabic barbarians halted when it was about a mile from the wall. It was tantalizing to see their mass, but they could not make out any details. Nabu knew how aggressive and heartless they were. They continued to advance at a slow creep. Queen Zenia would not charge until after the arrows were deployed. There was tension and anxiety as the sky turned from day to night with the approaching storm. The Babylonians wrapped their faces with heavy rags, ready to press forward.

Ahmed's warriors lined up on their horses, with the swords ready to lop heads and disendow many. They jostled for space as if in a tournament. The Babylonians were mainly on battle horses; others were on elephants, armed with javelins and poisoned-tip spears. There was a lull when it seemed like the fighting would never begin, the wind increased, and the horses were agitated, for the wind was strong and compelling, although the men were not.

The most dreaded of the powers in the desert were the seven Baleful, the spirits of the winds. The Magi had a pugnacious look. The patterns were indiscernible. Queen

Zenia looked at the Magi as a wind rose from the south, bringing whirling sand. The Arabic edged their fidgety horses forward.

The High Priest had managed to get on the roof of the Ésagila Temple. He could see Queen Zenia leading the troops. The city people stood on the ziggurat in the city's center, the gate to heaven, with bows and arrows. In the straight streets and Terrace of hanging gardens stood archers, ready. The city would usually be bustling with commercial activities, but today, it was covered with fearful silence like a pall. Like grasshoppers, the enemy troops could be seen making their way toward the city walls. Elephants were put on the last lines to stomp on anything that would fall.

The noxious winds swirled, lifting rocks and sand. A complete eclipse came upon the land as the day turned pitch dark. A bloodcurdling cacophony arose from the rebels. Snorts, squeals, and roars filled the air. Horses took off at the cries, drawing closer and closer. A battle cry went up from somewhere. A cheer began and was drowned almost instantly by the thunder of hordes. The battle was on. The sour smell of sweat and fear filled the air.

Thousands of arrows rose like a flock of birds from behind the walls. And the host of the Queen was mighty to behold, great and strong, and it covered the land like a cloud of grasshoppers. They launched with power and might. To her right, Nabu, and to her left, the Magi, and above them, the Babylonian flag flapping, whirling, fluttering, and whipping.

The sounds of men, beasts, horses charging and falling, battle cries, and, somewhere in that noise, the bones crushing and dreadful screams of men in agony that fell to the arrows that flew by day or stomped by the elephants.

The two armies battled, and the fight waged strongly. The land was a sea of blood, and the feet of the elephants were like pillars of coral. The mighty elephants bent their necks to the ground while they raised their horns like mighty bulls charging the enemy. Zenia's arm was strong, and her courage was undaunted. Arrows flew from the walls all day like rain and hail falling from a dark cloud. The surviving Arabic started to flee. Zenia and her army pursued after them, and the face of the storm was upon them. Still, when the Babylonians saw the storm approaching, they turned back, but the Arabic ran into it, and the destructive storm smote them.

When shouts of victory reached Ahmed's ears, he was angered and set to seize Zenia and the child, for he was a mighty man and terrible to his foes. He desired the bounty on her head.

CHAPTER TWENTY-ONE

VENGEANCE IS MINE

A tempest storm had devastated Babylon, destroyed the rebels, and left the inhabitants in awe. All was quiet again in the city, except for the distance chirping of night bugs, whistles, croaks, and ribbits. Queen Zenia stood on the balcony with hanging flowers. Few flowers were left after the storm's whipping, but the sky twinkled with lights flashing across the starry sky. She looked down at the babe in her arms, wrapped in a warm blanket. For a while, she thought she would never see him again. It had been a catastrophic day, and although all was quiet after the storm, her mind still had questions. Why did the Arabs try to ravage Babylon? They were allies. Who sent them and why? The city's walls were impenetrable; even the desert rats knew this. Did King Dawit send them to reclaim Babylon? If he did, why were they not equipped with weapons? Devastation and depredation had visited Babylon, but mercy and grace had chased them away, delivering them from the enemy's hand. Was it over, or just the beginning of tribulations? She wondered, not confident, for the Shah could be treacherous. Looking at the baby fidgeting, she sang a lullaby to calm him down:

Hush-lil baby,

Don't you cry

All the pretty elephants

Joined in the fight

When you wake up,

you will find

A pretty elephant by your side.

Ahmed Abul crawled out of his hiding place, gliding like a snake. His ploy to get into the city and the temple had worked. He slithered out from the inside of the statue and was in front of the serious-looking idol of Marduk.

He touched the idol, his eyes full of greed. "Pure gold," he whispered to himself. "Blaspheme, this is blasphemed, my friend, hoarding gold while my people starve." He climbed to the deity's side with a double-edged ax and a sharp dagger. His mind was filled with evil thoughts, and his heart was engorged with greed. He smiled behind the bashlyk when he reached the crown of the idol. "My friend," he said to the idol, "all this gold, but you can't see and speak, silent and blind, while my people suffer."

Large shadows cast on the walls as Ahmed stood on the crown of the forty-foot idol. The flickering illuminated his intentions to flinch, steal, and purloin.

The giant idol stood on a pedestal, symbolizing fertility and vegetation. It never provided for his people, Ahmed thought. He put the ax against the head of the idol, and like a fallen soldier, it bowed its head to the ax, crashing into thunderclaps that echoed in the peaceful night. Fragments of gold scattered unto the ground.

Gaia heard the sound, and a concerned look ran across his face. The sound came from the temple. He immediately went to check on the precious idols. The dim light obscured his sight as he entered the temple. He thought he had seen someone gathering gold pieces into a leather bag. It was not until he saw fragments of gold from the head of Marduk on the ground that he realized what was happening.

Others also heard the crashing noise, wondering what it was, for it was loud. Queen Zenia had just put the babe in the crib, and the sound almost woke him. *Were the storms returning?* She wondered.

Horrified by what he saw, Gaia entered the temple, demanding answers. "Who are you, and what are you doing in the temple?" he asked indignantly. Ahmed was startled. Gaia started to approach the man, his walking cane ready to defend the idols, when suddenly Ahmed took out a dagger tearing a slit through Gaia's tunic. Gaia was shocked. He staggered, trying to draw breaths in gasps. Gurgling sounds came from his throat, and he seemed unable to breathe as his gut poured out. He stumbled to the ground, bleeding from his mouth. Ahmed withdrew the long dagger as Gaia sank to the floor. Blood spurted from the wound; the flow slowed to a trickle. The evil man continued filling his leather bag and fled. "Now for the Queen."

The Magi had heard loud crashing sounds but would not leave his post outside the Queen's chambers. His duty was to keep watch of her and guard the child. The Queen called from her chambers, "What was the sound? Have soldiers go and inspect the temple," she said from behind the curtain. The Magi called for Naomi to stay with the Queen while he returned.

Ahmed had climbed the balcony where he had seen the Queen earlier, slithering in the dark like a thief in the night crawling on his belly.

Queen Zenia suddenly saw a man enter her chambers through the window. She reached for the dagger she carried strapped to her thigh, but she had put it under her pillow. Frantically, Zenia fought off the attack with her bare hands. The baby woke up with squealing, penetrating cries. Naomi ran into the chambers, sword in hand, to see a man attacking the Queen. She charged, but Ahmed was quick. He plundered his dagger into Naomi's chest, cutting into her heart. Her lifeless body twitched as it fell to the ground. Ahmed immediately launched at the Queen with all his strength, knocking her senseless. The last thing she remembered was the cries from the baby as she slid into the unconscious.

Now, King Dawit was delighting in the festivities, surrounded by an entourage of soldiers, nobles, and leaders. The crowds were in an uproar, gasping, as hungry lions were released into the arena. Gabe sat on the right side of the King, cheering with the noisy crowds.

Imam, an alpha lion, had just defeated Kopa, an undefeated champion, and Gabe was celebrating his winnings. Eagerly, he watched as two new opponents were introduced for the games. Kimba, the lion, was a ferocious beast that had defeated an elephant and a rhinoceros in past games. Gabe was excited and ready to place his bet when he saw Amber, the royal pet.

Amber was a three-year-old domestic female tiger— Queen Zenia's pet. There was no mistake; she had a mysterious marking on her forehead shaped like a black diamond and distinguished markings. Everyone in the palace knew she was the royal pet. What was she doing in the sporting event?

"That's Amber!" shouted Gabe over the crowd. King Dawit could not hear what Gabe was saying. He had not yet taken a good look at the tiger.

Amber herself did not know what she was doing there. She was perplexed and puzzled; where were her handlers, and who were these strange people who netted her and then caged her? What did they have to do with her? The tormentors had thrown her down and choked her repeatedly. Then, she had been left alone in a moving cage for several days, dazed and suffering from hunger. She could hear roaring lions not far away, causing her to spring on her padded feet several times, alarmed by echoes and shadows in the dark desert.

Four evil-looking Ethiopians approached her cage after what seemed like a long and tortuous trip. They laughed, poked her with sharp sticks, and made animal sounds. Amber's anger and hunger waxed. The Ethiopians gingerly pushed the cage to a larger opening, letting her out. Just when Amber thought she was free, she heard growling and snarling and saw a ferocious lion fast approaching. Amber sprung on her strong paws, her hair bristled and mouth foaming. The lion circled her. He quickly gained on her.

The crowds cheered, making her nervous and anxious. Both animals had been starving for days. The rule of the game was to kill and eat or be killed and eaten. One of them will become the meat for the other. Would it be Amber or Kimba? The bets were on. Amber was new to the games, but the spectators knew tigers were faster and more robust than lions; still, Kimba had earned his respect and was undefeatable.

Amber leaped into the air; her three-hundred-pound body launched at the lion. Kimba roared, sending chills up and down the crowd's spines. The crowds were on their feet with excitement. Amber's hind legs were longer than her front legs; she leaped at the lion from 10 meters, landing on his back, her large, curved claws digging into the flesh. Her canines, like blades, penetrated deeply into her prey; a large chuck of the lion's back was severed, which she swallowed whole.

The lion would not back down; he was a champion, and his pride would not be taken. His aggression escalated quickly. He threw her off. Amber leaped in mid-air, her jaws ready to close on the lion's neck, but Kimba was a pro; he dashed, clipping her front left paw. She had never fought a male lion. The wild goats she ever hunted were in the protected woods of the royal jungle. Occasionally, runaway slaves would invade her tuft and be hunted, but they were no match for her. She was dazed by the wound, crawling back to her feet, staggering and limping, blood flowing from the injuries. Her beautiful stripes were flecked with bloody slavers. Kimba advanced on her again, taking another chunk of her hind leg. All the agony Amber had endured was nothing compared to this exquisite pain. She let out a deep roar, sending vibrations that could be felt by the spectators, bringing them to their feet, including the King, for he recognized that roar. King Dawit noticed Gabe had left his side. Amber hurled herself at the lion, but Kimba was fast and shifted from the right to the left, coolly catching her under the jaw, wrenching downward and backward. Amber leaped in a complete backward circle, landing on her four strong paws. The proud lion would not have his pride taken from him; he was king of the beasts. He focused quickly, gaining on Amber's back. Her small clavicle was not a disadvantage; it gave her greater stride and a wider unrestricted range of movement. Her sharp canines penetrated deeply, sensing for nerves to sever. Kimba shook her off like a rag doll, throwing her. His claws grasped her stout. Amber's muscled body launched into Kimba, knocking the wind out of him.

The crowd roared, out of control, as Amber leaped forward, her tail balancing as she pursued her prey. Her teeth were drenched in blood. The proud lion fought furiously to get her off his back, throwing her on the ground with all his strength. Amber stumbled to her feet, profusely bleeding and severely wounded. She rushed

Kimba, but the lion shifted and struck a death blow, ready for the killing. Something distracted him. It was at this point that an ostrich was introduced into the arena. Kimba was no fool; an ostrich was easier prey than a tiger. He immediately pursued the docile prey, killing it instantly and devouring it. Amber's senses came back to her, but not her strength. She lay where she had fallen, watching as the champion lion feasted on the giant bird. The crowd booed angrily as Amber was removed from the arena.

Later that day, King Dawit paced back and forth, inflamed with anger. "Who has done this evil," King Dawit asked angrily. The four Ethiopians stood dumbfounded, as if their tongues had been cut out, paralyzed with fear.

The King was ready to sentence the four men to death when a messenger interrupted him. "The city of Babylon has been attacked, the temple of Marduk has been plundered, and Queen Zenia and the child are both missing."

CHAPTER TWENTY-TWO

ACCUSATIONS

The entire land lamented for Queen Zenia and the royal child. The temple of Marduk had been ravished, and his idol plunged. King Dawit took to his chambers for many days and would not see anyone. At the end of the mourning season, he decreed a court hearing on what had occurred in Babylon.

The King sat on the throne accompanied by his Royal Bodyguards, attendants, and servants. The Satraps also sat on their dais. The chiliarch announced the next respondent. "General Nabu, from Babylon."

A Median officer escorted General Nabu, carrying a wrapped carpet. Norman helped carry the heavy burden they both bore on their shoulders.

"What is this!" King Dawit shouted when the wrapped carpet was placed before his throne. He was already tormented and hoped it was not the body of Queen Zenia. An odorous smell filled the air. Mother Queen quickly covered her mouth and nose with a veil.

"Unwrap it," ordered Gabe, his face anxious. He observed closely. The odor was repulsive. Todd wondered if it was a dead camel. As Gabe suspected, it was a headless body, a male, not a eunuch.

Mother Queen sat on a small throne. She hoped it was Queen Zenia's body, but to her surprise, it was the body of Ahmed; she recognized the smell. It was the man she had hired to destroy Babylon and behead Queen Zenia. Her face paled with fear. Zenia had escaped.

"Those responsible for the destruction shall die by the sword," Mother Queen heard her son saying. Suddenly, she felt faint and, for the first time, afraid. Her son could have her crucified.

"The Hellenes did this, destroyed the temple of Marduk, and took the Queen!" cried Mother Queen, standing up. Her eyes flamed with fear. "Put ropes about their neck and a price on their heads, with hideous tortures!" King Dawit was vexed in fury. "I swear," he vowed, "those responsible for this will pay with their lives."

Dawit was twenty-eight, a young, guileless man with a simple heart, when he inherited the kingdom. He was a great military leader and was expected to finish his father's quest to conquer Greece and bring it to subjugation. Several internal conflicts had delayed his plans, but there was not a day that he was not reminded. He continued adding fleets to the navy and warriors to the military and constructed two significant projects, a bridge and a canal, for the grand campaign. He planned to campaign immediately following the Nowruz celebrations. His plans were already delayed. "Speak General Nabu," King Dawit urged.

Nabu stood looking guilty. He had been outwitted while he and his army lay inebriated when the enemy invaded and ransacked the temple of Marduk. He felt responsible, for the Queen trusted him for the safety of Babylon, and he had failed. The damage to the pyramid and tomb of the late King Nebuchadnezzar was extensive. The temple had been ravished, desecrated, and burned, but the missing Queen and her child could be tried as a capital offense. His future was uncertain, and his death would surely be long and tortuous.

"With their hearts full of greed and malice, they came from the deep sand sea, but Marduk delivered the land from their evil destructions by sending storms to devour them before they entered Babylon," said General Nabu. "In the silence of the night, after the celebrations were completed, Arabian spies hidden in the temple, within the bowels of the gods, rose and killed Gaia, the High Priest. They ravished and burned the temple. Immediately, the army sought for the enemies within the city, but none were found, and the Queen and child were also not in the city."

King Dawit listened empathically. "Come they from the deep sand sea? Were there Hellenes? Has anyone identified the body found in the Queen's chamber? Speak and hold not thy truth from me, for I am a gracious king, extending mercies to those I love but releasing wrath upon my enemies."

"My gracious King, it was a time of chaos. The land and its people were celebrating; many visited from different regions to honor Marduk; there were multitudes of people, and if there were Hellenes among us, I humbly declare, I knew not. The army came from the land of the Arabians, and they came to destroy Babylon."

Were there Hellenes among the Arabian army, the King wondered.

"Speak not out of fear, for no harm will come to you," said King Dawit, turning to Norman.

A dreadful fear came upon Norman, he looked disoriented, dressed in sack cloths made from goat's hair, and his face blackened with ashes. The tall, thin man stooped with the world's weight on his rounded shoulders. He cringed from the burning eyes of King Dawit.

"Speak!" commanded the King.

"Your Highness, my heart is grief, and my soul is heavy; it is difficult to say what happened suddenly. I heard the cries of the child and the screams of Naomi. I ran into the Queen's chambers with a dagger in hand and found Naomi, the Queen's help servant, gravely wounded on the ground. The angel of death came immediately." Norman wiped a tear from his eye, unable to continue speaking.

King Dawit lowered his eyes to hide his own emotions. The royal princes and officers listened attentively. Although cruel and cold, King Dawit was moved with compassion.

"The decapitated body was found on the ground, but the Queen and the child were not; it all came so quickly.

I searched the Queen's chambers and the palace and found not the foes nor the Queen. I ran outside to find the temple an inferno of fire and dared not enter into the consuming flames."

"Where were those who vowed to protect the Queen, the Magi?" asked the King.

"The fire devoured and destroyed two people. The remains we discovered in the temple were of Gaia, but we know not of the other bones. It could be the servant Magi," said Norman, gesturing.

"Speak, Woman, hold not thy tongue from me!" King Dawit said, focusing his attention on his mother, who looked pale. "Why do you suspect the Hellenes have done this evil?"

"Their animosity festered because you, my son, have failed your father's mission to subjugate the Greeks! Mother Queen said, pointing her finger at King Dawit. "They will not stop until the Ionian states are liberated from your rule," she continued, her eyes full of lunacy. King Dawit again looked away to hide his face, for he could not bear any more shame.

Mother Queen, however, did not hoodwink Gabe. Something was disturbing about her reaction when the body was unwrapped, as though she knew who it was. The decapitated body did not shock her, but something else did, and he wondered what. Gabe knew Mother Queen had been seeking around with Doctor Democedes, the Greek. The Doctor influenced her and did not support the campaign to Greece, his homeland. Something was afoot, but he was unsure and held his peace. He only spoke when he had something urgent, but all the King's leaders knew about her fears. Why was she accusing the Hellenes?

"You have waited too long to avenge the insults, giving the enemy time to reinforce their armies…now they come to collect a generous ransom for the queen's return," said Artabanus as he entered the courtroom. "Remove the stench from the presence of the court," he ordered, looking at his sister sternly. He suspected she was responsible for what happened in Babylon. Mother Queen approached him to go and hire emissaries to destroy Babylon. He warned her not to stir up a storm but thought it was clever how she blamed the Greeks.

"Why would the Hellenes take the Queen? They do not even hold their women in high regard. The Hellenes are preparing for the Olympic competitions," interjected Todd. "They are hard at training."

General Artabanus's penetrating eyes burned through Todd. He did not like others to disagree with him, including his son. "Have you any proof of this?" he retorted objectively. He wanted the campaign to the Aegean Islands to be on time.

"Dr. Democedes requested to be allowed to attend the competitions," offered Todd. "During this time, the Greeks practice peace, harmony, not war."

"Bring Democedes to me!" snapped King Dawit. An officer immediately left the court in search of the Greek Physician.

"Why bother Democedes with this?" Mother Queen asked, fearing for his safety. "Send Ambassadors to the Greeks and demand Zenia be returned," she suggested. "Do these wretched little people from yonder fear not the King of the land?"

Gabe was sure; something was amidst. Has she forgotten the last time envoys were sent to the Greeks, they were thrown into a pit?

"That's clever," Artabanus replied, surprising Gabe and Todd. We can send Todd, Mardonius, and Democedes. Secretly, he wanted them to bring back reports regarding the land, their military preparedness, and their weapons. He couldn't care less about the infamous Queen.

King Dawit adjourned the meeting, offered gifts, and promised to honor any royal prince for exploiting information regarding the destruction of Babylon and the missing Queen.

It was an Olympic year and a scorching day. At the heart of the games were religious festivals and gatherings of riotous barbeques. Todd was dressed in a simple chiton tunic sash, fastened with a cord belt and leather sandals. He felt exposed. How can men be comfortable not wearing trousers, he wondered. Democedes seemed comfy in his tunic, but Mardonius sympathized with Todd. Quietly, they traveled on miniature horses up a summit of unpaved and very steep terrains, deep gorges, and dry foothills covered with chaparral shrubs. They were heading to the third highest peak of Mount Olympus to the Temple of Zeus.

"Thousands of athletes, male family members, and countrymen travel on this difficult road for the competitions to the sanctuary of Olympia, situated in the northwestern Peloponnese. This is the birthplace of the Olympic Games," informed Democedes. "The temple is accessible to all people living in the different city-states."

"The temple adheres to the Doric Order. Zeus stands in the most severe style of Greek art," continued Democedes. "On metopes are the Heracles, Pelops, and Oinomaos statues in the battle between Centaurs and Lapiths, Hermes of Praxiteles, and Zeus and Ganymede. At the center, the statue of Apollo silently directs the battles and decides their outcome. There is also an agora, an open theater, an acropolis, and four gymnasiums." Mardonius was impressed by the chiseled statues depicting the human anatomy.

The path was lined with vendors in tents selling crafts, sculptors, poetry, paintings, and other artisans. "Are these craftsmen also part of the competition?" asked Todd.

"Yes, but they are here to compete in the artistic competitions, not the games," replied Mardonius. "Some of these poets will be commissioned to write poems praising the Olympic winners who will become legends for future generations. During this time, the city-states in the Aegean lands set aside their differences for the five-day celebrations. It's good for trade, military alliances, and politics."

Todd could see a pockmarked by olive trees. A group of workers cut leaves from olive trees and carried them up to the altar of Zeus. "Wreaths will be made out of these leaves to be presented to the winners of the Olympic games," said Democedes. From afar, the men could see the limestone temple with relief metopes of marble. "The marble is imported from the island of Paros in the Cyclades," Democedes proudly announced. The building sat directly on a stylobate, with both taller and thinner columns. The columns on its long sides were more than doubled on the short sides. There were six columns on each of the temple's east and west facades and 13 columns on each of its more extended north and south sides. The pediments were lavishly decorated with life-size sculptures.

A peddler dressed in a white tunic approached Todd. "Eros is written on your face, I have the perfect gift for your Aphrodite desires, and showed him a gold ring with two naked people embracing…" five silver coins a small value for thy beloved."

"You will see the most influential athletes in jumping, throwing, boxing, wrestling, pankration, and chariot racing for the five-day event," informed Democedes, shooting the peddler away. "These celebrations attract more than 45,000 spectators from the different city-states.

The stadium only holds 40,000," said Democedes with an impeccable smile. "The games are intended to bring peace, harmony, and unity to the people." Todd noticed many distinguished men, but where were the women?

"Although the conflict between the cities is ubiquitous, it is within the interest of all city-states to engage in these games. The people rely on each other for political and military alliances. The games are good for revenue and serve as platforms for representatives of the city-states to compete against each other peacefully. Most influential athletes become prominent leaders within their city-state," said Democedes. A school of eight-year-olds dashed up the steep mountain. "We are the mighty Athenians, second to none. We are number one!" they chanted in unison.

"Is that General Theodore?" asked Mardonius, looking at the prominent man surrounded by dignitaries, who stood before a sumptuous tent splendidly decorated with furniture and entertainment. "Yes, a statesman from Athens. A disrespect to the great families. A man without a title, eager to acquire riches. He likes to draw the distinguished circle of friends, seeking glory for his achievements," whispered Democedes.

Two strangers walked by, talking about horses. "He threatened to turn my horse to a wooden horse with false litigations," one said; the other stopped and stared at the man with the sage hair, recognizing him from somewhere.

"Where are the women?" Todd asked. He had heard the Legends of Troy and wanted to see if Greek women were as beautiful as Helen was portrayed. "Women are not allowed to compete...there was one exception, a young princess named Cynisca, a Spartan princess. But later on, you will see female performers and entertainers," Mardonius said.

A distinguished man with a group of athletes huffed and puffed up the steep hill. "That's King Leonidas of Sparta," informed Democedes, a descendant of Hercules.

"Hercules?" laughed Todd, tugging on his tunic.

The men passed a montage of activities: schools of naked boys running up stone roads, towering ivory statues, sanctuaries, animal sacrifices, charioteers, oxen lining the streets, ambitious politicians, and wealthy patrons. Still, the most eye-catching was the huge nymphaeum served by an aqueduct. Todd stopped to listen to a blind orator recite verses from The Iliad of the Odyssey. 'My name is Nobody. The blade itself incites deeds of violence. And empty words are evil. Each man delights in the work that suits him best.'

They were nearing the tent Democedes had reserved with food, drinks, and lodging for the men. Todd had never been to a gymnasium but was told by Democedes that it was the best place for gathering information.

The gymnasium was a sanctuary—walled around a large courtyard on the city outskirts. The athletes ran for distance during training as they would during the games, in a double Doric colonnade divided into two tracks. The main outer track was called the ksystos, and the other was the auxiliary track. Next to the main structure was a prominent court used for javelin and discus training. In the center was the statue of Zeus.

When Todd arrived, the gymnasium was crowded with athletes, warriors, and trainers. Philosophers were in discussions in another part of the gymnasium, where musicians played music. He was astounded. The room was full of shameless, unrobed men, exposing their athletic bodies. Before the Greeks, the men anointed their bodies with oil, offered animal sacrifices, and spoke oracles. Every city-state had its own God, but Zeus was the King of all the other gods, an angry god that hurled lightning bolts down from heaven.

The athletes were warm and hospitable, shaking hands firmly and smiling. Their bodies were a work of art, with balance, lean, and robust muscles. Todd was amazed at how healthy and strong everyone looked. The Persians needed to be healthier looking. Todd was distinguished, taking after his father and uncle—a giant, strong, handsome man with cinnamon skin and stunning grey eyes. In competing games, everyone who met him admired his skills, noble appearance, and swiftness in strength.

An older man, greying at the temples, approached Todd. "Good early morning," he said with a warm and welcoming smile. He offered a handshake. "My name is Aristotle, from the land of Stagira."

Todd shook his hands, "Good early morning, he replied in perfect Greek. I am called Todd."

"I believe our paths have not converged; I cannot recall your face," said Aristotle.

"I am from the land of Thessaly," Todd answered.

"Ah, the language of Sappho," said Aristotle, clearing his voice. He sized Todd, sensing something was wrong. "Are you familiar with the greatest female poets from the island of Lesbos?" He tested to see if Todd was from Thessaly.

"The Tithonos Songs. Eos, the goddess of Dawn. Sister of Helios, the sun god who crossed the heavens by night in her chariot, drawn by two winged, white horses, shining her silvery light," replied Todd. In his poetic flair, he recited:

Sunrise is the color of a love-made

Real lifelong lovers know this to be true

A color that can never-ever fade

Like precious Bavarian Danube Blue

Each dawning always being different...

Doctor Democedes had schooled him well. Every Greek city-state had a story about their local gods, which the inhabitants knew. He sensed Aristotle was testing him. Dr. Democedes watched the interaction between the two men from a distance.

"My trainer waits on me," Todd lied. Democedes was lifting stones. He started to excuse himself, but Aristotle was not done scrutinizing the handsome stranger.

"Do not be so hasty; will you join me and my guest for a symposium dinner? I hired a host from Syracuse to bring traveling performers, girl flutists, acrobats, and dancing girls. There will be plenty of meat and wine. The guests will be champions from Iberra to the Black Sea," he said, smiling. "My hospitality is extended to your companions," he said, looking toward the sage-haired man, who looked familiar.

"Make haste then; I accept your hospitality and will propose it to my companions," said Todd. He worked his way through the crowd toward Dr. Democedes.

Mardonius busied himself watching a wrestling competition between an Athenian and a Spartan warrior. The massive men covered in oil combined boxing with wrestling. There were rules; they could not attack the male genitals. There were no points, no time limits, and one of the fighters was much smaller than the other. They had to indicate their surrender by raising their index fingers. They fought till one felt exhausted to the ground, and the other stood above him in the conscious grandeur of victory.

"You must not engage in idle talk; your dialect will betray you," said Democedes, looking around. Key politicians gathered around Theodore. "Listen, if they hold the Queen and the child for ransom, someone will say something."

Democedes whispered to Todd. "Conversations topics include philosophy, politics, and gossip."

"May wisdom guide my words and cause me not to stumble," said Commander Theodore.

Theodore was a populist who supported the lower-class citizens of Athenians, a new breed of non-aristocratic, who rose to prominence and propagated democracy. He had increased Athens's naval power, awaiting the Persians' invasion. In his youth, Theodore rebelled against the distinction between noble and baseborn. He liked speaking his mind in council meetings, with his blade-sharp tongue stirring up hatred. Famed for valor in strategies and an active mind, he was always ready with a clever plan to meet challenges.

The most incredible thrill was the amphitheater filled with spectators to see men and women face death against huge charging bulls, a lusty sport.

General Theodore drew a large crowd. He opened his lecture with an invocation to Zeus. The commander looked at the men gathered. "Sons of Greece, the stone that freedom stands on is in the sea. The serpent of Minerva has disappeared; the goddess has left the city and gone toward the sea, where the battle cries are heard. I cannot fiddle, but I can hear the great cry. Strike, if you will, but listen. We should trust in walls of wood and ships for the great fortune of our states. With the Dawn of the day, salvation comes from the sea. Act, speak, and think as one who knows that, at any moment, the barbarians can arrive at our coastlines. Remember, in Hades, there are no offerings to the gods. Be wise and prepare to defend your city-states and earn the honor that lasts forever among men. If you live three thousand years but throw away your courage and join not in the liberation of freedoms, you perish in the end, and no fame will be found in honor of your name."

"The lifetime of man is but a point, a flux faint perception and dull," cried an old man. "The Athenian leader encourages more fighting. Cheers, cheers!"

"The strong do what they have to do, and the weak accept what they have to accept," called a tall man in his mid-twenties with long curly locks and bright green eyes. *"The two most powerful warriors are patience and time; cheers, cheers!"*

"Many people will not take the trouble to find out the truth but are inclined to make a stand accepting the first story they hear!" said King Leonidas. "Fear is a reaction, but courage is a decision; cheers, cheers!"

Theodore continued, "We must stand up to the invasion that wavers in the shadows of peaceful times."

It was late afternoon. The Ambassadors dressed in long white flowing robes and garlands on their heads attended another assembly. The discussions centered on democracies, a subject Todd did not wholly understand. Only male citizens could attend and participate in the assembly, but Dr. Democedes got them in. A people that would govern the land, *what makes them think they have the right to govern themselves,* thought Todd. *Did not God appoint the King to deliver humans from chaos?*

Many of the orators spoke in riddles and parables, yet in all their speeches, not one mentioned the Queen. Finally, Dr. Democedes stood up to speak in the assembly. "We come to seek a peaceful solution," he said. "King Dawit laments over Queen Zenia and his child. He has asked me to soothe the quarrel between Persia and the Hellenes with peaceful talks. Or he will lead the armed army to carry out his orders and attack."

"Why, that is preposterous!" spoke King Leonidas in defiance. "Has the King gone mad? Come ye here to accuse us of stealing your Queen...have we not enough women in our lands to populate the world!"

"Surely some disease of the mind has seized the King. The earth and the skies will not bow down to this insult," cried General Theodore.

"We are messengers of King Dawit, offering peace to a delicate problem. This is not an insult. Have you the Queen and the royal child?" asked Dr. Democedes.

"We have not the King's trophy nor her child. King Dawit is mistaken and misguided to think we have time for foolish tactics. We know nothing about what he speaks of," said King Leonidas.

The following day, Dr. Democedes was absent from the camp. Todd and Mardonius searched for him, but he was not found. In haste, the two men left Athen, fearing the Greeks had captured him and would come for them next.

The back of a man with sage hair stood looking out an open window. "It has been years since the Achaemenid Empire has campaigned against the Greeks, but they will come to rescue the Queen of Babylon and the royal child. Make haste, and prepare to fight."

"Why come he to us? We bear no blame for the Queen of Babylon," said King Leonidas in his booming voice.

"Allegations were made that the Aegean kidnapped the Queen, King Dawit demands her return."

King Leonidas paced back and forth. "King Dawit violates the warrior ethics, and if he comes to our coastal lines, we will be waiting."

Meanwhile, outside the Susa Palace, the sunny sky became gray. King Dawit watched in silence. It was an eclipse, but none of the astronomers had mentioned it to him. He called the astrologers to interpret the phenomenon.

"It is the foreshadowing of a battle that has been long-standing between Persians and the Greeks," a Magi reported. That same night, King Dawit had a vision, an apparition of a tall, handsome man. "Beware of making war on Greece," he said. The Shah woke up in a cold sweat and had problems falling asleep. He left his chambers and went to the women's hall, seeking a concubine to comfort him.

CHAPTER TWENTY-THREE

PATHWAYS

Rosie walked behind the Susa Palace, sneaking behind large, glazed brick columns, shading against walls and bushes as she discreetly worked around the traffic of diplomats, emissaries, Persian satraps, and ambassadors, seeking an audience with the Great King. Many came from distant places, with gifts and tribute from taxes of the subject people. Dressed in a brown tunic, the watchful eyes and ears of the King did not know it was Rosie. She knew better than to be outside the harem walls without an escort, but something was wrong, and Rosie needed answers. The Shah had returned early from the Nowruz celebration and would not hold court for many days. The servants dared not to speak of the missing Queen, her child, or the destruction of the temple of Marduk for fear of

Mother Queen, who would have anyone skinned if she heard any rumbling about it.

The spies dispatched to the Aegean Islands, accompanied by Dr. Democedes, had returned from Athens. In the absence of her doctor, Mother Queen's health had declined, and the growth on her breast looked infected. She had been calling for her doctor. Rosie awaited his return, for she did not trust the enchanters and healers; their magic never healed anyone.

Quietly, Rosie found the courtyard around the palace's surrounding walls, lashing with gold, electrum, and ivory. There was a succession of many gate-towers and gateways, separated by many stades of fortified brazen doors and high walls; on the outer side, most eminent men were drawn up as personal attendants to the King himself. They were guardians on each exterior wall, listening and watching. The King, who had the name of Master and God, could almost see everything, or hear everything, but they could not see Rosie. The Faithful Six gathered with the King inside the inner chambers behind the courtroom.

Rosie pressed her ear to the stone walls outside. She recognized the voices of Mardonius, Artabanus, and

Todd, but who were the other three, and where was Dr. Democedes?

"May the King live forever in the land," greeted Mardonius, King Dawit's older brother. "What news do you have this morn," asked King Dawit. His face tensed, his aquiline nose up in the air, and his large eyes creased with thick eyebrows. He sat clothed with strength and military prowess. His thick hair and beard resembled Ahura Mazda, but no god was he, for he was cruel.

"Ye have heard our brother Democedes has fled to Croton, where his countrymen now protect him," Mardonius informed.

"Dr. Democedes abandoned the royal family," Rosie whispered to herself. That's worrisome. Mother Queen's reactions could be catastrophic. She feared for the young maidens in the harem, who were undergoing the cleansing rituals in preparation for the deflowering by the King. The head eunuch, Haggai, had to be notified. It would be devastating if Mother Queen became raged and disfigured the virgins being groomed for Queenship.

King Dawit's head was filled with wind when he heard the news. "The man with the sage hair served the royal family well, yet uncontented was he with royal tributes?

Still, has he betrayed the hand that protects him? I pray he does not snare his limbs across the desolate waste." Dawit was less concerned with Dr. Democedes. "Hold not thy truth from me," he said eagerly. "Does the Aegean hold Queen Zenia and the royal child as ransom?"

"Men of the Aegean Islands are senseless and impure, following the lies of Ahriman, perverse of heart, they cover not their loins and worship many strange gods. They seek many consultations, night and day, they ponder. Gold and silver, they endear and betray thy brothers for riches. But the bribes offered did not produce witnesses of the Queen nor the child." said Mardonius, clearing his voice. "However, numerous islands among the discord people could have the Queen." He was treading on ocean waves. None of those spies planted within the Greek leaders were inclined to the Queen; something so scandalous would be known to the leaders.

It was hazardous business being in the King's good favor. Even the central authorities were highly scrutinized for behaviors of transgressions or treason. Dr. Democedes' fleeing could be considered treason, and Mardonius could be held responsible.

"Savages of eloquence, they speak in parables and fables," interrupted Todd, fearing for Mardonius. "They speak of a serpent, Minerva, who disappeared and went toward the sea. There is much talk of walls of wood and the dawn of salvation from the sea. What is the meaning of this? I know not."

"The land is plentiful with devaes," added Mardonius, encouraging the conversation to be redirected. "Unrobed men anoint their bodies with oils and sacrifice animals to strange gods. They also speak of a demokratia government. The goddess Minerva is the devaes of the sea.

"Fortresses, city walls, and roads they do not build, they pride themselves on the display of nudity, at the temples, plazas, gymnasium, and they practice cowardly and foppish behaviors," added Todd.

King Dawit wondered how his father had been defeated in the Battle of Marathon. Only savages could live that way. He will champion them and provide security, peace, and justice so they can prevail. "We shall lead a military expedition against them, rescue the Queen, and subjugate the remaining cities," he announced confidently.

"The channel across the Hellespont at the base of Mount Athos Peninsula in Chalkidiki is completed," reported Mardonius, glad to change the conversation. "Two triremes will be able to pass for mobilization of the navy."

Rumors of war had been circulating for eight years, and nothing had happened, but Rosie feared the King would mobilize his expansive army against the Greeks to rescue Queen Zenia. That would be devastating, for the King would want the harem to travel with him, and what if the Persians lost the battle? What would become of them on foreign soil? They would become spoils of war to be sold, raped, or killed because the Greeks did not hold women to high standards.

The harem girls were rigorously watched, and no outsider was allowed to see or visit them. When journeying from the palace, they were transported in carriages called harmamaxa, covered with curtains around the four sides. Todd watched the approaching royal carriages with the harem girls. He knew touching or seeing one of the royal concubines could cost him, but he did not care for his life. Amara was on his mind. It had been months since he had seen her. The maidens got out of the carriage individually, with the help of eunuchs, who were allowed around the virgins. He thought it would lift his spirits if he could see Amara one last time before he was deployed back to Greece. He may not see her again. It had been six moons since Amara was brought to the harem.

Kaleb, her uncle, had been dismissed from the King's inner circle and placed outside the palace as a watchman. Mother Queen punished him publicly and had his head and beard shaved for entering the Harem's Hall and trying to sneak Amara in without her notice. It was humiliating for Kaleb, but a minor penalty for a capital offense. *"Where was Amara?"* Todd wondered. Identifying her was difficult. All the girls had their faces covered. Lurking from behind the wall, he asked how to send her a message. He had to let her know he was deploying to the Aegean seas and did not know when or if he would return. Suddenly, his attention was drawn to a eunuch in a brown robe hiding behind pillars and walls so as not to be seen.

Todd was curious. He was one of the King's eye, investigating suspicious behavior. The eunuch quickly walked down a small road in the outer garden, pushing through the crowds to a dark courtyard of heavy foliage. Todd saw him go behind a bush and disappear into a crevasse in the ground covered with forage. He followed the eunuch down a hollow hole in the earth. It was an underground path that led to a corner in the garden of the harem. The hole was cleverly concealed under a bed of flowers. Todd found the brown robe on the ground, but the eunuch had vanished.

The beauty rituals for the virgin maidens continued undisrupted, even with the rumors of war. Rosie ensured since Mother Queen had taken to her bed with illness.

Vanessa watched with hawk eyes. She was Amara's helpmate and secretly prayed the King never honored her with a silk handkerchief. Eunuchs were assigned to give the maids special oil massages to perfect their limbs and beautify the contours of their faces. Oils pressed from sacred Asian plants protected their skins from the scorching sun. The maidens wore transparent veils and loose clothing during the day, but by night, they disrobed in their bed, allowing healing in the natural air. Fowl eggs and wheat flour paste were applied weekly on their faces to remove blemishes and smooth the skin. Their long tresses were treated with plants from India to deepen the color and thicken the hair. Amara was becoming more and more a royal princess by the day. She was wise and full of grace. The eunuchs and the maidens favored her above all the others, and she was given a double portion of clothing, jewelry, and treatments.

Todd sat in the hole in the earth, quietly watching as young maidens danced around the pool while others played, chasing each other. Todd's eyes scanned the girls, looking for Amara. Where was she? He could hear music playing from a harp. The girl playing was surrounded by greenery and beautiful flowers. He could not tell if it was Amara, but the girl playing the music was beautiful. He could hardly believe his eyes, for the damsel was beauty to behold, like an angel from heaven. After a while, he recognized her; it was Amara, but she was not alone; three helpmates were with her. One of the maidens he recognized. It was the Ethiopian girl Vanessa, who had been caught drinking the haoma drink in Pasargadae.

Mother Queen was nowhere in sight. Todd put on the eunuch's brown robe and quietly crawled out from under. No one was watching. Slowly, he walked toward Amara. His heart throbbing inside his chest; how could he get a moment with her? It had been six moons since he last saw her, and so much had happened, but he knew she had not been deflowered, for her period of rites had not yet been completed.

Amara looked up to see a eunuch approaching. It was not Haggai, the head eunuch, who was short and stubby, ebony black with incredibly thick lips. The eunuch must be new. He was tall, young, and walked as one with authority. His grey eyes were penetrating. It reminded her of someone she knew. As he got closer, Amara gasped, her mouth opened. Was it the ghost of Todd? She had heard Todd was sent as an emissary to Greece. Amara dared not make a sound or say anything, but the hawk-eyed Vanessa saw Amara's face as if she had seen an apparition. Amara wanted to be left alone while she savored the moment, quickly dismissing the maidens to go for refreshments. The other two young maids left, but Vanessa was reluctant; something had happened to Amara, and Vanessa thought it was an unusual request to send her away.

"Worry not for me; go, the teacher of songs comes to instruct," Amara said to Vanessa. Her eyes were trance-fixed on the approaching apparition. Vanessa quietly left but did not go too far. If anything happened to Amara, she would be held responsible.

Todd seemed to flow toward Amara, and she wondered if Vanessa had given her haoma to drink, causing visions. She looked at the apparition for a long time, who suddenly reached for her hand, brought it to his lips, and kissed it. Amara stood shaking; not a word was spoken. The air filled with the songs of rhyntace birds. A soft, tender breeze caressed her cheeks, Amara's eyes filled with tears. "Are you the angel of Todd?" she asked.

"My beloved," said Todd, "I have searched for you many days, and finally, Ahura Mazda has bestowed on me a path that I may glance at thy beauty." It was not an angel; it was Todd.

"My uncle brought me to this dreadful place, but what is this eunuch I see?" said Amara, unable to bear the pain that he had been made into a eunuch, to be with her, or how else was he allowed in the harem?

"Cry not, it is not so, for I have found this cloak, and a path has been made to come and see you. But I must not tarry for fear of being discovered," he said, looking around cautiously.

"Tarry not, come again before the curtain of the sun rises, and we shall meet in the privacy of my chambers at the center of the garden," Amara said, pointing toward her chambers.

Todd thought he saw someone approaching and froze. His face turned pale like a ghost. If caught in the harem, he could be beheaded. Amara looked to see Vanessa approaching fast.

"Quickly, you must leave now," urged Vanessa, giving Todd a questionable look. "Mother Queen approaches."

Todd smiled at Amara and fled like a thief. The two girls did not see where he had disappeared.

"Who is this eunuch that causes thy cheek to rouge?" asked Vanessa when they were alone.

Amara looked at Vanessa, benumbed. Was her contentment so apparent? "That's the eunuch of music," said Amara, not wanting to reveal her private matters, for in the palace, the walls had eyes, the trees had ears, but whoever would love life and hoped to see good days must keep their tongue from evil and their lips from speech.

CHAPTER TWENTY-FOUR

THE CORONATION

The Monarch needed to appoint a successor before he ventured to risk his life in foreign campaigns. The Shah was not equal to his father, for he had yet to produce an heir for the crown. King Dawit had two sons born of commoners, Hystaspes and Dararios. Their mothers, two concubines, had strong and bitter quarrels about who would be the crown prince. Any child born to a concubine was regarded inferior and illegitimate, and the King could appoint a close of kin, like General Artabanus, Mother Queen's brother, General Mardonius, his brother, or Todd, his nephew.

A sea of people prostrated on their faces before the throne of King Dawit. These people were soldiers, military officers, and Royal Princes. The King surveyed the multitude of people. At age 39, this King warrior had not gained his military carriage nor practiced his mind, always listening to poor advice. His arrogant face was etched with stress, eroded by strong drink, secret unhappiness, and lust for women, especially Queen Zenia. Mother Queen also sat in the queen's seat. She was bedecked in full ceremonial clothing and jewelry. Her long hair was in donut braids adorned with golden pins. At 50, she was still a beautiful woman with finely chiseled features and a turned-up nose, showing the long line of royalty, but like a Sphinx, she lacked luster in her eyes.

The congregation of people all rose silently, facing the throne. The sun had not yet drawn its curtains, and the heat was already fermenting. The army formed a canopy over the King and his mother. Behind the right hand stood the two young princes, already warriors in character, with aquiline noses and masculine good looks set by the Great Darius. One of them would become the successor to the throne if King Dawit did not return from battle.

A slight motion from King Dawit brought Gabe to his side. Dawit asked a question. Gabe bowed and looked toward the side door to the room. On his face came a strange expression, a kind of indecision as if he dreaded what was coming. The young princes exchanged looks between them; they suspected something.

Hystaspes was 14, unwarlike, soft, and gentle, and kept himself secure surrounded by eunuchs and women, but Dariarios, 12, had a broadening smile and lived a prudent life, second to none. He was a seasoned hunter and warrior who had accomplished many noble deeds in his young life. The princes have been well groomed in the court of the King to become leaders of the largest Dynasty known to man.

Outside the palace, the sounds of running horses and chariot wheels punctuated the silence.

"The winner of the lion hunt will be the chosen prince." King Dawit said with a peculiar, strange look of shame, for he had already chosen a prince whose grave was unknown, and his name forgotten.

The King led as he did in war, and his men followed. This was basic training for the young princes, rising early to harden for the endurance of heat and cold. Run to the top of mountains at a fast speed. Let their arrows fly and javelin ready for quarries crossing their path and be sharpened in spirit by dealing the stroke as the creature closes. Stand guard when rushing; if all fails, hand to hand, with a dagger.

The horse riders rode out, splendidly attired, Persian courtiers and the army's elite. Every one of them was a sight to behold, but the most impressive was the King himself; he was riding a powerful and striking Nisaean horse whose trappings, bit, cheekpieces, frontlet, and breastplate were all gold; he wore a mantle of Tyrian purple made from Babylonian cloth, and his tiara was the color of hyacinths; he had a sword at his waist and carried two spears, and slung over his shoulder was a bow and quiver of the finest Chinese craftsmanship. He was an impressive sight on the saddle.

Soon, the mountains were full of people shouting and running, dogs barking, horses neighing, the game in fleeing excitement, and the noise would have driven men out of their senses; delight was mixed with anguish, joy with fear, danger with enjoyment.

King Dawit took the reins strapped to a chariot, leading the hunt to a narrow entrance that penetrated a short distance into the hills, ending in a sac of cliffs, huge rocks, and caves. This was where the lions breed and live. And the place was swarmed with them. Lions came into action at the approach of the chariots. Some scattered running, and several of them moved toward the box, the mouth of the canyon. This group was led by a large male lion who sported a tremendous black mane. He leaped up onto a great rock out of reach.

It was the custom of the royal command that no one should pursue the game until the King threw the first spear. But Dawit did not permit this interference. He wanted the boys to enjoy the hunt and let all his comrades give chase and try to outdo one another, each doing his very best! He watched from his position as they rushed upon their animal foes, vying eagerly with each other in giving chase and throwing their spears. He was delighted to see the young princes unable to keep silent from delight, but like a well-bred hound, he hollered when an animal came close and urged on each of his sons by name. The King was delighted to see Hystaspes laugh at one and laud another without jealousy.

Dariarios looped his reins around his hand and took his bow and a handful of arrows. Almost immediately, the team of horses had to pull itself up, rearing, pawing the air as they arrived at a rock barrier. A vortex of actions with roars and dust whipped up to the apex of excitement.

A lion leaped from a rock directly over his chariots. Dararios turned to look, having practically felt the lion as it went over. The black-maned male leaped, jumped past, and rushed out of the canyon. The prince grabbed the reins, pulled his team around by man strength, and set out in pursuit. The black mane leaped out and streaked across the plains. The chariot emerged. Streaking across the plains again, the lion disappeared over a ridge.

Hystaspes was in a small area of clear dunes. Atop a hillock was a shrine, a small shaft the size of a camel's needle. Foolishly, the lad got out of the chariot and kneeled at the base of the shaft. He looked frail, handsome to the point of prettiness, ascetic, and almost in a trace of reverie. The sounds of lions were distant to him. Dariarios sees the lion approaching his brother; he turns his chariot around. King Dawit also saw the foolish boy on the ground, gathering wildflowers. Hystaspes was in great danger, for the lion could easily tear him apart. The King whipped the team to intervene between the lion and his son. With a bow and arrow in hand, he took a shot at the lion over the back of the horses but missed. Dariarios' chariot arrived just in time and veered off the lion, but the chariot was overturned, spilling him out into the ground.

Gabe watched through the film of sand dust thrown up by the smashup. He whipped the team around and took a shot at the lion, but the lion was too fast. Dariarios looked to the east with tense expectancy and took a dagger out of his belt, plundering it into the chest of the leaping lion. He was furious at his brother and yelled at him. "Ye idim!"

He rushed to quiet the team and right the chariot. Equally angry was the King. "Do you know you could have been killed," he said, his eyes burning with intense anger.

In a voice that had a strange, delicate quality and given an added strangeness by choked intensity, Hystaspes replied, "The rim of the sun is just beginning to show over the horizon, and it's time to pray."

King Dawit reacted with astonishment; was the lad a priest? A team of soldiers on horses hurried to Prince Hystspers and carried him to a chariot. Dararios prize was enormous; he could not believe he would be the successor to the throne.

The Zoroaster Priest presented himself with a mace, the Varza, and a steel rod crown of a bull's head. Administrators, Chief Authorities, Satraps, Generals, and the King's vassals traveled to Pasargadae. They gathered in the temple of Anahita, the goddess of royalty and war, to witness Prince Dararios' installation ceremony.

King Dawit ruled many people with different customs, laws, religions, and languages. Still, Ahura Mazda was the god who bestowed and legitimized the Kings as elected representatives on Earth.

He was not the firstborn, but his bravery and hunting skills had settled his succession to the throne. Dararios was an Achaemenid, hereditary of blue blood. The young lad had no understanding. He stood looking at the massive assembly of people who came to witness his rite of passage to Kinghood. Nervously, he looked around. Someday, he would have sovereignty over all these people, yet he stood dressed in a dirty old shepherd's cloak.

The Priest stood before the Prince. Dararios held a baby lamb, a gift from Mother Queen. He had been tendering the ewe for the past week and had grown fond of it.

Behind the Priest followed seven eunuchs. The Priest poured consecrated oil over the young lad and the baby lamb. "Ahura Mazda himself, a divine warrior, empowers the King with the strength and skill to fight in battles and bring about the truth created at dawn," he said.

"Cyrus the Great started caring for the goats and sheep of lords and kings of those days. His only meal was pistachios, dried figs, and spoiled milk," said the next eunuch.

The next eunuch took the ewe and gave Dararios pistachios, a brick of dried figs to eat, and sour milk to drink. "The Achaemenid Empire started with humble beginnings. The cloak you are covered with was worn by Cyrus the Great," he said.

At that, the lad stood up straighter; the cloak had taken on a different meaning.

Another eunuch lighted an oil lamp that had to burn day and night until the young prince's death. "May the light guide your steps."

The next eunuch said, "Ahura Mazda created the King as a friend to right, not a friend to wrong, and bestowed wisdom and strength on him that he holds his own in battle as a good horseman, a good bowman, and a good spearman."

"The royal insignia presented belongs to the throne," said the sixth eunuch, placing a long scepter on his right hand and a blossom of lotus on his left.

The final eunuch brought the crenelated crown, royal clothes, and smooth shoes without laces. The eunuchs surrounded the lad and dressed him. Then, they carried him to a throne similar to the King's but smaller.

A Magi inspected the liver, the soul of the sacrificed lamb. He looked first for the caput iocineris, the head of the liver; it would be a bad omen if that part were missing. Then, he looked at the colors and shapes in the tissue. Were there any growths or strange cells? The middle or finger of the liver was critical; it determined whether the prince would bring forth good crops from the earth. The different branches were porta gates.

The dignitaries patiently waited, and finally, the Magi looked up. Dararios was mesmerized and anxious. *Was his future unveiling?* He wondered. Everyone was eager to hear the report, especially King Dawit.

"You shall be known as Artaxerxes. In five years, the son of King Dawit, Artaxerxes, will have a great name. He will rule with the specter of peace and justice. The porta gates will remain neutral, but there springs a root whose fruits will bear witness of greater things to come." That was a strange reading, the leader and dignitaries thought. All believed except Artabanus, who had different plans for the future.

CHAPTER TWENTY-FIVE

MOBILIZATION

The Persian invasion was a delayed response to the defeat in the Battle of Marathon. It was already late Spring when they started the march from Susa to Sardis. To avoid the scorching heat, the army traveled in the dark sky. Sacred oil lamps illuminated the Royal Road on which the King was carried. Warriors, including the ten thousand Immortals, one thousand cavalries, a collection of harems, servants, shepherds, eunuchs, and livestock, traveled with the Shah. General Artabanus, a robust and confident warrior with keen eyes and military prowess, led the caravan.

Haggai, the head eunuch, had convinced King Dawit to leave the royal harem in his care during the campaign to Greece. "Traveling with the harem would be cumbersome for the young maids, nursing children, and pregnant women," he told the King. Reluctantly, King Dawit agreed. The harem was especially important to him; the women, however, rejoiced with songs and dancing when they heard the news of morn. The maidens would be unsafe in a hostile land where they would be treated poorly and risk becoming tools for trade or bargains, especially if the King lost the battle; they could become spoils of war.

Todd had visited Amara in the harem again before he was dispatched to Sardis. He did not know when or if he would return from the battle. On King Dawit's birthday, he planned on asking for her hand in marriage. He put a little gold ring on her finger—a reminder of his promise to love her even in death. Inside the ring, he had inscribed, 'I am my beloved, and my beloved is mine.'

"Weep not for me, my beloved, for God is a lamp unto my feet and a light to my path," Todd said as he tenderly kissed her forehead. "Nothing shall come between us; my love for you will not wither even in death." Amara's tears flowed silently; it was yet another loss for her. For days, she took to her chambers, not eating nor drinking, and would not allow the Sun to grace upon her. The beloved Vanessa comforted her through the valley with stories and songs.

Mother Queen greatly feared for the safety of her son. Even though it was clever of her to blame the Hellenes for taking the Queen and her Bastard child, she was endangering the life of her son. His blood will be required of her if he dies. King Dawit had to return safely.

The Magi reviewed a book with symbols and signs when Mother Queen entered his quarters.

"Your Highness," he prostrated before the majestic woman. "What is the honor of this visit?"

"I am weary and heavily laden for my son's safety," she said, weeping. "What recommend thee to ensure my son returns safely from the battle?"

A contempt look came upon the Magi as though he knew something. Mother Queen wondered if he could see into her dark soul.

"My lady," the Magi said, after a while of silence, "Would ye allow me to craft a court robe of protection for the Shah?"

"Thy wise one, I would be indebted for eternity." Mother Queen answered, kissing his hands. The Magi was surprised by her reaction.

He wasted no time, for the army was a week from marching. The Magi weaved wool from a young lamb into a large double square. Using gold, white, and purple silk thread, he made a motif of gilded hawks attacking each other with their beaks.

On the morning of departure, Mother Queen visited her son.

"My moon-faced son, the Sun will not shine upon my quarry until I see my son return from battle. I am heavy with grief," she cried in his arms.

"Fear not for me, Mother; I hear no man can truly be happy until he dies." Mother Queen started wailing and crying, for she had sent her son on a treacherous journey with falsehood and greatly feared the outcome, but still, he needed to finish his father's unfinished business.

"I bring a gift for my moon-faced son," she said after a while of being in her son's embrace. She gave him a wrapped cloth.

"What is this, My Royal Highness?" The King took the gift and unwrapped the beautiful, elaborate robe.

"Put it on, my son," Mother Queen urged. "It will protect you from the storms that rage by day, the arrows that fly by night, the songs of the sirens, and your enemies."

"Fear not, my lady," said King Dawit. A knock on the door interrupted their tender moment. It was her brother. "We are ready," said Artabanus. The King kissed his mother's hand and left.

King Dawit slowly advanced his vast army and a large fleet. The army was well provided for, with three thousand ships full of grains, food, water, and all the necessities for his men. For the first part of the journey, the army marched northwards through the land east of the Tigris toward Nineveh. The Gyndes and Zab rivers had to be crossed by ferry, landing in Amenia. The route continued through Cilicia and turned north through Cappadocia to the River Halys—the borderline of the Croesus empire.

The army consisted of 60,000 troops, which took a week to ferry them across the Halys. They arrived at Sardis by Autumn. The late King Croesus's palace was in a walled acropolis; Dawit resided there for the winter months.

In the following year's Spring, the Persian troops were ready to continue their mission after the Nowruz Holiday. King Dawit conducted a review of his troops when he reached Doricus in Thrace. The army set out from Sardis was more extensive than when he set out of Susa, as he continued to add warriors of Medes, Elamites, Babylonians, Phoenicians, Judeans, Egyptians, Bactrians,

Scythians, Sogdianas, Lydians, Cushs, and even Indians from the far eastern edge. Together, they band with a few contingents of soldiers recruited by local rulers to form a colossal army.

The leaders were the twelve brothers and half-brothers of King Dawit. Mardonius was a high commander, as well as Artabanus and Todd. Artemisia, the ruler in Caria and half-sister of Zenia, would join to fortify the Navy of twelve thousand triremes and three thousand ships from Phoenicia, Palestine, Egypt, Cyrus, and Cilicia.

General Hydarnes commanded the infantry unit with the elite Immortals. They traveled with their food supply, livestock, camels, oxen, and servants. Their collection of harems traveled in covered wagons, shielded from the leering gaze of private soldiers. Among the women was Yoko Shun. She had been given as a wife to Hydarnes, for her beauty was exceptional. Her maimed feet did not take away from her, and she won the heart of Hydarnes. She was also an exceptional warrior.

"After the Nowruz's celebration, we will move towards Hellespont," informed General Hydarnes, a rowdy man with battle scars.

General Artabanus briefed his army: "Troops will be levied in all the satrapies, and the navy will be the supply line for the warriors. The traveling harems will not surpass Sardis, for the oceans are unstable, and the fleets will only transport warriors to the mainland of Greece."

The Persian forces were two hundred thousand troops divided into units of ten thousand with the same backgrounds, uniform language, and similar skills. The multi-national bands used their own distinct weaponry and fighting styles. These armies had never trained together.

The Persian and Median armies were clad in colorful sleeved tunics and trousers, felt caps, and fish-scale armor, and each carried a bow and arrows as well as a spear and a dagger, with a wickerwork shield for protection. Other groups like the Kissians and Hyrcanians were armed similarly to the Persians. These troops included Assyrians, Bactrians, Scythians, Indians, Areians, Parthians, Chorasmians, Gandarians, Casptians, and Asian groups. Then there were Arabians with long swords, fastened at the waist with belts, dressed in zeiras.

The Ethiopians dressed in leopard and lion skins with their bodies painted in white and yellow. They carried bows and poison arrows tipped with stone instead of bronze. The Libyans wore leather and carried javelins, daggers, small shields, plaited helmets, and sturdy boots. The army from Asia Minor had similar weapons: javelins and swords. Greeks from Ionia and Mysians also carried javelins. They joined the military after crossing the Hellespont and wore brightly colored zeiras.

The elite army wore long robes with wide sleeves and appliqued badges, all in yellow and blue, woven headbands, and their shoes were yellow leather in the Persian fashion without strings. They also wore masses of gold jewelry, torques, and armbands, marks of honor at the Persian court.

Before the Royal Army crossed the Hellespont, King Dawit paused at Troy, offering the goddess Athena a thousand cattle. Many of the Mene warriors thought it was a mistake, especially Gabe.

"See not the handwriting on the wall?" Gabe asked King Dawit. "The extravagant sacrifice had led to fear and terror among the followers of Ahura Mazda."

Gabe had been with the Royal family since King Dawit was a stable hand. There were things he stored in his heart, but he had convictions, for only Ahura

Mazda appointed Kings, and Dawit made offerings to daevas, creatures of shadows, spirits of the lie. Whispers circulated among the warriors, "The King is guileless and simple-hearted…his eye is not open to the envious daevas who seek to destroy him; where are the seven angels who watch over the King?" This stirred much anxiety among them.

Pythius of Lydia, the second richest man in the world after King Dawit, helped finance the war and offered the King four million gold darics. The Shah would not be outstaged by anyone and matched the amount from his treasury. King Dawit took much pride in giving, not receiving, a traditional trait among Persian nobility. Pythius, however, was astute and intended to ask the King for a boon. He had consulted the celestial sky and learned of a coming eclipse that was a bad omen for the King. Fearing for his sons who were in the military, he asked King Dawit to allow one of his five sons to be excused from military duty so he would take care of him in his old age. This made the Shah upset and anxious.

"Look at the massive army I have, and all are slaves to me, even the royal princes," he barked at the old man. "I will spare your sons, but one will become an offering to cleanse the army," he added. Pythius could hardly believe how full of rage and hate King Dawit was. He begged for his son's life, but in the end, his oldest son was cut in two halves, and the Army marched between them as they parted from Lydia.

"This is not the behavior of one appointed by Ahura Mazda," wept the old man. "You are following the path of the Lie!" he shouted as the Army marched on. The old man cursed the ground the King walked on.

Just as the army marched between the halves of Pythius' eldest son, there was an eclipse of the Sun. The Magi interpreted it as a good omen for the King. "The Persian army, the Moon is about to overwhelm the Greeks, the Sun," he professed. But the old man Pythius knew and laughed like a madman when he saw the sky.

In the narrow channel of the Hellespont, the Shah had built two bridges of 300 ships tied together by a network of robes. Two bridges anchored off ships faced the Black Sea, the other bridge sweeping down from the Marmora to the Aegean. Lines ran from Abydos to the coast opposite Bigal Fort and Nagara Burnus to the headland south of Bigal. This was the narrowest part of the Dardanelles, where the currents were faster and more turbulent than they were to the north, making it more complicated with sharp bends in the straits just west of Abydos. The engineers had picked a spot where the water flow would be less hostile to ships for a distance of eight stades. Once the ships were anchored, cables of flux and papyrus were stretched from one shore to the other across the top of boats. The wires were constructed in Situ, using capstans to twist the fibers into ropes. The brushwood trees were cut and sawn into planks, laid across cables, and covered with earth to resemble a road. Palisades were erected on the edge of the planks to allow men and beasts to cross the roadway, shifting less than if it had been fastened to the ships. A bulwark was erected on each side of the causeway high enough to keep animals from taking flight at the sight of the sea.

It was an excellent plan, but a violent storm arose that night; the winds and the sea tore the ships from their mountings, causing the cables to snap. King Dawit, known for his anger, became annoyed and frustrated, ordered the execution of the chief engineer, and had the sea flog three hundred lashes.

The army was delayed another month, unable to cross, but the false interpretation of the Magi's reading had the King swelled with confidence like the waves of the untamed sea. "The Greeks will surrender without a fight," he boasted, his eyes glaring and sparkling. That night, the ruling family of Thessaly sent a mission encouraging Dawit to take over the Aegean Islands. King Dawit took this as a sign from God and was carried away by emotion, prestige, honor, and the desire for revenge and punishment.

In the early summer, the army reached the friendly Greek territory of Macedon and halted. The fleet and army rejoined at Thermae and began their journey south into Greece. King Dawit was confident as he slowly advanced. Many Greek city-states remained neutral, and others joined with King Dawit.

The Greeks had plenty of time to prepare but were not united, bickering among themselves. The council wanted to defend the Vale of Temples, but others preferred relying on the Wall at the Isthmus. The Spartans formed a general alliance with several city-states, agreeing to stop all wars among themselves and unite to protect land and sea.

King Leonidas, in his late sixties, was a formidable warrior. He was the son of Kleonymus, from the royal family of Agiadae, and was chosen to lead the combined

Greek forces. The Spartans would protect the land, and the Athenians would protect the sea. They had to work corporately to coordinate their defense points. Sparta initially wanted to protect the narrow Vale of Temple between Macedonia and Thessaly. The idea was abandoned after they realized it would work against them. Athens was left to their faith, with open borders. When Theodore heard there was no barrier between Athenians and the Persians, he immediately proclaimed, "Every Athen citizen should save his family as best as he could." Some Athenians fled to Aegina, some to Salamis, and others to Troezen. Men of fighting age were conscripted into the navy as crew members for the fighting fleet. Women, children, and older adults rushed to the ferries evacuating the city. Amid the commotion, a man shouts at the fleeing people, "Surrender, surrender to the Persians, surrender and live!!!" A group of angry women went to his house and stoned him and his family to death. "We fight until we die," cried the women in agreement.

'Why sit ye here? Fly, fly to the ends of creation. All ruined and lost since the impetuous fire speeding along in the Syrian chariot hast to destroy her.' The air was full of dread with the approaching Syrians. People rushed with a few things and their families. Schools of young children carried the older men to the departing ferries. The tame animals followed their masters to shore. Howling pets filled the air when the overladen vessels drew without them. One little dog named Lexi leaped into the sea, swimming alongside the ship. She paddled until she reached the island of Salamis, where her master had landed. A six-year-old freckled-faced boy cried, "Lexi, Lexi!" rushing past the crowds of people. He runs to the dog, lying on the ground, gasping for air. She slightly wagged her tail when she saw her master. Her body was convulsing and trembling from exhaustion. "Lexi, Lexi," cried the little boy, picking up the little dog. "Lexi," he cried. But the little dog died in his arms. "Mommy, mommy, pray Zeus to bring her back," he pleaded.

The Greek leaders decided to protect the pass of Thermopylae with 7,000 hoplites and 271 triremes at Artemisium in northern Euboea. They intended to halt and damage the Persian forces.

Sparta, the dominant military powerhouse, was celebrating the Carneia festival, a tribute to Apollo. General King Leonidas immediately canceled the celebrations to prepare for the battle. He selected three hundred elderly men from the allied states as his task force. The men had to have living sons to carry on the family line. Delegates were sent to every city in the Peloponnese to beg for troops or supplies. Many cooperated.

Meanwhile, King Dawit was having strange visions. "Take care not to consider visions senseless, for they are divine messages," Artabanus warned. The King had been visited by an apparition who showed Queen Zenia in the land of Theni with the Hawk people.

"God did not just create the world; God created happiness for mankind," said the King, his eyebrows creasing, and his long, curly square beard elegantly displayed, giving the appearance of deity. His quest in life was to subjugate the Greeks and regulate them, for they were out of control.

"Seasons have come, many moons have gone, and much time have I dedicated in preparation for the day of revenge for the Battle of Marathon. I have not followed my father's path, and it's time to face the Aegean and champion the land," the King answered Artabanus. "This is something I must do." His unbridled arrogance expected the winds and waves to obey him, for he was the representative of Mazda Ahura.

"The Greeks wage war extremely unintelligently and fight on the plain until everyone dies instead of using deception. We will win," chimed in Mardonius.

"God does not allow anyone but himself to feel pride," answered Artabanus as he looked at his reflection in the water. He also had a hunch that God was not with them.

CHAPTER TWENTY-SIX

THE BATTLE OF THERMOPYLAE

When the Persian Army reached Macedon, King Dawit sent emissaries to seek a peaceful solution before launching a full invasion.

"Surrender the Queen, the child, the land and sea, for it all belongs to me by the power of Ahura Mazda," King Dawit wrote.

The messengers immediately left on a goat path, zigzagging up a hill. It was a steep, narrow climb with dangerous bulging rocks. Nearly half the road was decayed, and the animals were forced to cliff edges. Soon, they had to help each other, urging the donkeys from behind. When the messengers finally arrived, they were greeted by General Theodore, an assertive, impetuous man. He laughed when he read the scroll.

"The King thinks he has claims on Greece. The man has a disease of the mind," General Theodore said. "We know nothing of this Queen of which he speaks, and the grains and its ears of the Athenians will not yield to him."

Not wasting any time, General Theodore replied to the King.

"Son of Darius, there are two paths before you. You may choose which one you will follow, but you do not appear equal to your father. Your fame will not live long if you stay in this fight, but if you return to your home, you shall live long, even to old age, but your name will be forgotten. Putting men of thine own people to death, commanding them on charges of no truth, are not deeds of renowned valor for a King. We know not of the Queen and the child of which ye speak, but as for our land and sea, we will not surrender what the gods control." The General was a strict disciplinarian and trained his Army to fight for the ideals of freedom. Dimokratia was a ravenous desire to him, and he devoted much time and strength to the cause.

"We are not sentient puppets and will not subjugate ourselves into slavery, for in doing so, we will become lost in the world, surrendering our wills and souls to a ruthless taskmaster. We will not be drained of the morality of volition like dead leaves in the wind. We will fight as long as our bruised bodies can stagger forward." General Theodore told his men, who were the best and bravest in the land.

King Dawit sat on a gold throne, enjoying his meal. His men gathered around him. There was leek soup, lentils, fried spinach, peppery green, tareh, leg of lamb and plenty of royal wine. When the messenger returned, the King was dipping flat bread into a goat stew. A eunuch played a lamenting song on a chalkou and stopped when the messenger prostrated before the King. The Shah smacked his lips, satisfied, reached for his gold wine goblet, and drank as the response was read. After a moment of silence, he started to laugh. "Dare those wretched stiff-neck people profane my commands...! The General will not hold his head up at the edge of my sword."

The Persian fleet and army rejoined at Thermae and began the march south into Greece. The King was full of confidence on his first encounter with the Greek military, relying on superiority in numbers. He was warned in a vision that Queen Zenia was not in Greece. However, the

Shah wanted to conquer the fragmented Greeks to prove himself a mighty warrior.

The Shah led the vast Army overland from the Dardanelles, accompanied by a substantial fleet moving along the coast. He quickly seized northern Greece and began moving south.

The Persian army marched overland through Thrace and down into Macedonia while the fleet hugged the coasts, avoiding the storms of the Aegean by passing southward through a canal dug by force labor across the Isthmus at Mt. Athos to the length of a mile and a quarter.

Athen set out a fleet that sailed north to meet the Persian armada, and Sparta dispatched a small force led by King Leonidas. This small force gave Leonidas the added advantage of speed for the march of 360 kilometers from Sparta to the pass of Thermopylae, a journey of ten days.

The two navies met at Artemisium off northern Euboea. When the Greek admirals saw the overwhelming number of the enemy's vessels, they were minded withdrawing. Resistance seemed insane; the collection of Greeks was not even a tenth of the forces from Persia unless they worked together with a single mind and heart.

All day, the rival fleets fought until night, ending the engagement before either side could win; the Greeks then retreated to Artemisia and the Persians to Aphetas.

The Shah began the operation. On the first day, he sent a detachment of 200 ships, unseen by the eyes of the Greeks, to sail around Euboea and secure the narrows of the Euripus Strait. The Euboeans, fearing a descent of the Persians upon their shores, sent commander Theodore a bribe of thirty talents on the condition that he persuade the Greek leaders to fight. Theodore paid sailors to inscribe messages on rocks to the Greek commanders in the Persian fleet, begging them to abandon or deflect but not to fight against their motherland. He hoped his words and safe grace would move the Ionian Greek admirals.

Another monstrous storm rose the next day and wretched 200 Persian ships off south Euboea. King Dawit was entirely oblivious to the signs and warnings in dreams.

"They will fight to the end, Shah. Look at them; they are fearless," observed Todd. Secretly, he admired them, for they were a tenacious people with ideas of freedom and self-rule. Could it be possible, he wondered, for men to govern themselves and not be controlled by monocracy?

When King Leonidas and the three hundred arrived at the passage of Thermopylae, they repaired the old Phocian Wall to protect and defend the access.

Dawit halted at sea for four days, watching the Greeks repair the wall. He laughed at their efforts. "They will be severely punished once I gain control," he said to Todd, who watched in amazement. The massive Persian Army did not scare the Greeks to submission.

The delay gave the Greeks time they had lost, allowing the advancement of more troops from Sparta toward the pass. Their forces were 7,000 hoplites. The Greeks' strategy was to halt the Persian progress on land at the narrow pass of Thermopylae and in the sea near the straits of Artemisium long enough to starve the Persians into going home by intercepting their food supplies.

It was a suicidal battle, and the Spartans knew it. They devoted time to exercising, grooming their long hair, and sacrificing to their god, Apollo. Such an insouciant display of confidence enraged King Dawit.

The two forces faced each other in Thermopylae. It was a five-mile stretch from west to east, with mountains on the south and the sea to the north. The defile between the mountains and the sea was only a few meters wide and punctuated by three gates. This constricted the battlefield to prevent the Persians from utilizing their vast numbers.

The Greeks took their position at the 'Hot Gates,' sheer cliffs to the left and sea to the right.

King Dawit commanded the Greeks, "Surrender your arms!"

"Come and get them," replied General Leonidas.

The armies were so different in appearance and fighting styles. The Persians wore tight trousers, long tunics, leather boots, and caps. They were padded with jerkins and carried wicker shields. Their chief weapon, the bow, intended to wipe out the enemy by aerial bombardment before the cavalry were dispatched.

The Greeks took their hoplite phalanx stand, a block of heavily armed infantry standing shoulder to shoulder. The men wore heavy metal breastplates, kilts, greaves, and helmets and carried a spear and a short thrusting sword. They formed into a tight block impenetrable to assault and would steadily advance like a gigantic rugby scrum, trampling and crushing whatever stood in the path.

King Leonida prayed his men's hard training and discipline would give them victory in the battle, but if it didn't, it would fulfill the oracle spoken, 'A king has to die to save his people,' was he that King?

The Persians launched arrows, darkening the sky, but the Spartans took shade under their bronze shields.

The Mede army, not trained in hand-to-hand combat, was deployed next. The Greeks started to move steadily and deliberately, thrusting their long bronze swords at anything that moved. The Medes' spears and shields were not designed for confined spaces like the Greeks.

From King Dawit's point of view, he could see his army being butchered by the Greeks. Things were going differently than planned. He deployed a light cavalry of his finest and strongest warhorses. These stallions were bred and raised specifically for war, but the cavalry relied on the initial bombardment of arrows to cause massive casualties. The riders, high on their horses, would then charge in with swords, lopping heads as they swept over wounded foot soldiers. The ground was difficult for the horses to maneuver, and the riders became targets. These living, breathing creatures refused to charge the phalanx coming toward them. As in the Battle of Thymbra, the horses became alarmed and disoriented, throwing their riders off.

King Dawit jumped to his feet when he saw his horses falling to the edge of the swords and his men mauled over. He started to shriek. Gabe calmed him down.

The Immortals' troops foiled the cavalry. They were trained in guerrilla warfare. For two days, the Greeks defended against Persian attacks and suffered light losses, but King Dawit watched in horror, fearing for his army.

The battle took a detrimental turn. Todd was leading a small detachment of the Immortal Infantry behind a mountain when he captured a local Hellene, a shepherd. Fearing his family would be killed and his daughters raped, he showed Todd a secret route over the towering mountains on the backside. They descended toward the plains behind the Greek position and outflank them.

Despite Leonidas' heroic resistance, the Persians were upon them; retreat was not an option, for he was a Spartan, and it would defy his laws and customs. He moved his three hundred men into the broader part of the pass to deploy simultaneously. That morning, he had told the warriors, "Eat a good breakfast, for tonight we dine together in Hades." The soldiers offered sacrifices to the gods, and the little force moved forward in deadly silence.

The battleground was a confined space, and the saturation of soldiers caused the Persians to trample their comrades. The Greeks fought recklessly, disregarding their lives using swords when spears were broken. At the end of the onslaught, all the Spartans were dead, including King Leonidas. One survivor hanged himself for shame.

King Dawit went to assess the damage. Twenty thousand men were killed, including his brothers, Abrocomes, and Hyperanthes. The news of the defeat reached the troops at Artemisium, and the Greek forces retreated, allowing passage into southern Greece. King Dawit led the way with the head of King Leonidas fixed on a pole as a trophy for all to see, causing outrage among the Greek military leaders.

CHAPTER TWENTY-SEVEN

DEATH HAS A STING.

The land mourned with the cries of mothers, wives, and concubines, for their warriors were no more. Early before the rising of the sun, a squadron of soldiers carried two bodies up a steep hill through the gates of the Tower of Silence.

Mother Queen sat on a gold and silver throne; her face covered to shield from the rotting stench. Vanessa held a parasol to shade the Queen from the hot sun, who anxiously awaited the Magi's caravan. Another harem girl swapped flies away from her. Court attendants surrounded Mother Queen. To her left stood Kaleb, Amara's uncle, and to her right stood Rosie, her helpmate. Haman, the Master of Ceremony, announced the approaching soldiers.

On the outskirts of the gates stood the widows, mothers, fathers, and sisters of the fallen soldiers in the Battle of Thermopylae. *Where were their bodies?* Some wondered. Only two bodies were escorted, and many wondered *what happened to their loved ones.* Some knew their warrior would not have eternal peace because of how their bodies were treated. Others were too numb to think their futures were uncertain, for their husbands were no more. Some would become marketable for a living; others would become temple prostitutes. If they were lovely to look at, they could be sold by the head male relative, fathers, sons, or brothers. Then there were the angry ones, who had enough of the monarchy abuses and secretly hoped the King would be defeated by the Greeks to put an end to the abusive monarch. Wailers, both men and women, lamented in their cultural rituals.

Music of lutes and reed pipes was heard from a distance. The sun had not lifted its curtain, casting shadows of rainbow colors in the twilight of dawn. The air was perfumed with the sweet smells of incense and rotting flesh. People from all tribes and nations gathered, lamenting the death of loved ones. Some customs rented their garments, others tore their hair and beards, and others cast themselves upon the ground, offering prayers, libations, and animal sacrifices. An old man who had lost two sons fell upon the ground, rented his garment, took a razor, and broke out wailing.

The assembly was loud as each grieved the death of their warrior in their customs and rites. A squadron carried the bodies of the two royal princes up a very steep mountain. The people became silent as they passed by.

Their bodies would not be buried, for it was an abomination that defiled the earth with its impurities. The corpses would not be burned; the fire was sacred, representing Ahura Mazda in the material plane. Nor would the bodies be thrown into rivers, lakes, or oceans, for water was also sacred and should not be defiled with the impurities of human waste. The bodies would be isolated to avoid the impurities from evil forces that would invade them after death and dwell within. The spirit of Ahriman, the evil one, had infused the world with corruption. The only way to rid the planet of these evil spirits, called Nashuh, was to dispose of the body correctly. The flesh had to decay untouched or disturbed by living people after the rituals.

The soldiers prostrated before Queen Mother. "All rise," she said, her nose in the air and raising her right hand. There were no signs of grief on her face. Her son, King Dawit, was still fighting a raging war in Greece, but many had already died, and the battle was not over.

Mother Queen handed a scroll to the gray-bearded Magi. He read it, cleared his throat, and whispered something to the other Magi. They exchanged a puzzling look.

The Magi, dressed in long white robes, wiped a tear from his eye before speaking.

"Death levels everybody, whether he dies as a king on the throne or as a poor man without a bed on the ground," he said. Then, the Mages lifted the bodies individually and placed them on stone slabs in a corner of the towers. Their hands were arranged upon the chest crosswise. The bodies were placed north and their feet south. The ground had been dug out a few inches in depth, and a layer of sand was spread over it. The bodies were then placed on the spot prepared. After placing the bodies on the slabs of stone above the ground, the Magi drew three deep circles on the ground, called kashas. Everyone knew it meant a rest place, stay away. After having thus placed the body on one side of the room, the two priests left the tower still holding the paywand and finished the rest of the Srosh Baj. The following process was that of making the sagdid. This consisted of making a sag, four-eyed dog, or a dog with two spots just above the two eyes. The faces of the bodies were exposed to the rays of the morning sun, and on the fourth day, the souls would ascend heavenwards, but if the rays did not shine upon their faces, they would be doomed for eternity in the underworld of shadows. The sagdid (prayer) was repeated as long as the bodies were in the house. After the sagdid, fire was brought into the room and kept burning in a vase with sandal fragrant and frankincense. It was believed that burning fragrant wood over the fire destroyed the invisible germs of disease in the direction in which the wind carried the fragrance. The bodies were left to be devoured by the beasts of the air.

Another Magi informed the family of the prayer rituals. "These you must do in the morning and eve four days. The prayers offered are for solace, protection, and the journey for the soul toward Haurvatat or Ameratat… from the Sachkar until the Chahrum at dawn on the fourth day."

The red-bearded Magi recited: "Death and decay cannot overwhelm the spirit. Nashun corrupts all life. O

Holy Zarathushtra! If one carries with purity for the fire of the plant Urvâsana or any other fragrant tree, the fire of Ahura-Mazda goes to fight a thousand times against the invisible evil daevas in all the directions in which the wind spreads the fragrance of the fire."

The vigil was almost completed when nine innocent children, both boys and girls, were brought forth.

"My child," cried a broken and wretched young woman from the crowd. Another cry was heard, and soon, there were cries of multiple voices of women crying for their children, who were on the platform with royal soldiers.

Mother Queen stood up from her throne. "Fear not for thy child, for they will be offered as libations for the royal princes."

The people, including the Magi, the priest, the rabbis, and even the eunuchs, were horrified. The cries from the children and the people were punctuated with screams and wails that could be heard throughout the land.

Enraged with anger, the wailing old man stopped; he picked up a large rock and threw it at the Mother Queen. Soon, others joined, and before you knew it, a rebellion was in full force; rocks, bones, trees, and anything the crowd could get their hands on were hauled. Mother Queen feared for her life when she was hit by a large rock that knocked her off the throne. She fell as if dead, bleeding from the head. Rosie immediately shielded her with her own body to protect her. Vanessa paled with fear and found protection behind the parasol. Haman carried Mother Queen to her covered carriage for safety, but the people stood shoulder to shoulder, blocking the pathway and not allowing the caravan to move. Kaleb and a group of soldiers used horses to break them up, but the people were relentless. Kaleb was knocked off his horse and almost mauled by the people. They would not stop until the children were released. Mother Queen's carriage was set on fire and would have been burned alive if it was not for Hamen, who rescued her from the flames. The children were set free.

CHAPTER TWENTY-EIGHT

THE BATTLE
OF SALAMIS

The Persian Army had invaded the path of Thermopylae through central Greece. They raided, burned, and looted Doris into Phocis, like locusts causing calamities as they went from city to city.

The Shah and his cohorts set camp on the Areopagus, bombarding the city of Athens with burning arrows. General Theodore had evacuated the city, but a small group of priests remained behind to protect the temple. The priests could see the Persians trying to climb the almost impossible steep mountains from their view. They started rolling boulders down the hills that took off, bouncing and spinning as they rapidly increased speed, crushing the enemy forces. When the barbarians tried to climb Mount Parnassus, thunderbolts came rushing from the sky, breaking two crags off the mountain, causing an avalanche, killing many more, while others fled, fearing phantoms. King Dawit started to doubt that his army could siege them. Were the gods fighting for them? He wondered. Many had been questioned and tortured for information, but none knew of the whereabouts of the Queen of whom he spoke.

Todd discovered a route to the Acropolis beside the sanctuary of Aglaurus on the east face of the rock, and they reached Athens. As the priest saw their area invaded by the Persians, many despaired, and some threw themselves from the cliffs to their deaths. The forces destroyed and plundered the sanctuary of Apollos at Abae, setting the adorned city with spectacular temples and statues of the gods in flames. It was a cataclysmic destruction.

General Theodore's childhood nightmares had come to haunt him like a revenant from the past. The destruction of Athen devastated him; he wondered if he had made the right decision and relinquished his command to Edward to mollify the Athenians, who urged that he take the lead. The Hellenes were disdained to follow Theodore, for he was a theatrical tragedy. A ship from Tenos had informed him the Persians were amassing in the straits, blocking the Greek fleet.

The future of democracy was in peril. The gales off the coast of Magnesia had slowed down the Persian fleets, destroying several of their ships, but had not stopped them. Theodore withdrew to Salamis. He needed to think fast and strategically. The Greek Admirals were ready to flee, terrified at the number of ships sailing their way. They were outnumbered, but Theodore was confident in his fighters; yet, he feared being abandoned by his allies. The Athenian Navy had two hundred ships and would fight to the end, but the cowardly leaders wanted to open the Athen Harbor, giving access to the sea that would block the shipment of resources to the islands. How was he going to get the barbarians off the land and sea?

Theodore called an assembly of Greek Admirals on the island of Salamis. "Brothers," he said, gleeking as he spoke. "We are much more experienced at sea than the barbarians. Do not be in turmoil by the multitudes of ships nor brilliantly decorated figureheads who boast shouts of terror on us. We must despise all and rush upon the foes, grapple with them, and fight to the bitter end!"

Captain Architeles, who did not have money to pay his sailors, was eager to sail home. "This is ludicrous; see what we are against, and the men labor without wages."

"Why are you not paying the sailors?" resounded Theodore, his voice echoing. His reaction incited Architele, who feared his crew would go against him. "I have talents of silver to pay the fighting men," said Theodore, giving him a bag of silver. "Pay the men, or I will publicly denounce you for stealing from the crew." Theodore tried to keep the fighting men intact to support the battle.

He raked the Admirals with piercing, penetrating eyes to persuade their hearts and minds. "Do not forsake me in the middle of the battle," he said passionately, "I also fear, but I warned you that the Persians would return with a vengeance. We would be better organized if we were not constantly bickering among ourselves. The gods themselves have been helping us with this battle. Do you think for a moment that we have come this far to die as cowards? This is what we have been planning for the past eight years?"

Commander Edward, a childhood rival of Theodore, stood up. Their issues stemmed from boyhood when a flirtatious girl hoodwinked both boys. He was the fleet commander of Sparta but faint-hearted in times of danger and wished to hoist sail and make for the Isthmus, where the infantry of the Peloponnesian had been assembled to build a wall. He looked at the other Admirals. "What are we going to do? The Persian Navy outnumbers us two to one. I have repeatedly accused Theodore of being a danger to the established order, but in this case, I support him. It was his bright idea to build two hundred more triremes," Edward said, "I do not favor evacuating the island of Salamis and fleeing. To evacuate Salamis would give the Persians the Athenian Harbor, a gross act of leadership. We must not surrender the sea to the barbarians." Secretly, Theodore had offered him bribe money if he stood in the battle. The Athenian leader did not have public money. Theodore ransacked Piraeus and discovered an abundance of cash hidden away, which he confiscated to provide rations and wages for the battle.

"May I remind my fellow brothers of the oracles of Delphi," said Theodore. We knew from the prophecy that the city of Athenians was doomed, *'why sit ye here? Fly, fly to the ends of creation. All ruined and lost since the impetuous fire speeding along in the Syrian chariot hast to destroy her.'*

"That's why I evacuated Athens, leaving it in the care of Athena. But olive branches offered to Zeus appeased, and our prayers for a better future were heard. '*Safe shall the wooden wall continue for thee and the children. Wait not for the tramp of the horse nor the footmen, mightily moving over the land, but turn your back to the foe and retire ye. Yet shall a day arrive when ye shall meet him in battle. Holy Salamis, though, shalt destroy the offspring of women when men scatter the seed or when they gather the harvest.*'

Theodore had a clever thought. "The wooden wall is a metaphor for ships, which we used to evacuate the Athenian people before they perished. Why would the oracles of Delphi call Salamis Holy and not cruel? Does it mean that the men who are to die are the Persians?" he suggested, pacing back and forth. "We must fight them by the sea at Salamis, the last piece unconquered in Attic Territory."

After a long debate among them, the League called for a vote and decided to defend the Isthmus wall, contrary to what Theodore proposed. He was beyond himself, "You want to build a wall!" he cried in rage. "Then I shall take my two hundred ships and my people and sail to Italy. You can defend yourselves. That's exactly what I will do if you do not back me on this. I am finished; my land has been destroyed, and I am not willing that my people should perish also!" he cried in rage.

"Do not be so hasty in taking your forces away," said Edward. He knew the Greeks only stood a chance to fight the Persians with the help of the Athenian Navy; they had the bulk of the ships; the League only had one hundred and sixty-five in total.

"What I have said is what I will do; if I am not going to be backed up, I am fleeing with my navy and people," he said, a warning tone in his voice. He left outraged.

The League members knew they did not stand a chance without Theodore's support if they wanted to remain independent.

Theodore was not being unreasonable. He tried human reasoning and spoke of the miracles and signs from heaven and oracles, but still, they opposed him. The last thing he did was introduce a bill providing that the city of Athen be entrusted for safekeeping to Athena. The military embarked on the triremes after sending their children, wives, and servants to safety. It had been a time of lamentation and weeping as their loved ones sailed in one direction, and the soldiers traveled in the opposite direction to the island where the enemy would be fought. Many would never see their loved ones again.

It was a clear starry night, the full moon illuminated reflections on the opaque ocean. General Theodore watched the lunar tides. The weight of the world was on his shoulders. He had begged the Hellenes to go up into Boetia, gain the enemy, and stand there to defend Attica, as he had gone by sea to Arteminisum. Still, they clung fast to the Peloponnesus and were eager to collect all the forces inside the Isthmus, building a rampart from sea to sea. It was not the first time his suggestions had been rejected, and he felt betrayed, discouraged, isolated, and alone to fight a myriad army.

Most Greek leaders were distressed; some neither wanted victory nor understood what safety could mean. They had seen the devastation the Persians had suffered in the sea storms but could not see how they could win. Many of the city-states had already surrendered, and their supplies were being intercepted by Persian ships. How could they survive winter without supplies and grain to feed the people?

An old prisoner of war from Persia and a good friend of Theodore stood by him. "What am I going to do?

Sicinnus?" he asked, emotionally. Sicinnus, with droopy eyes, looked at him with compassion.

"Play the King's game," said Sicinnus. "Force the Hellenes to fight. Turn their worst fears into real threats, and they will fight with eagerness and ambition; naturally, they must fight if they cannot escape the enemy." That gave Theodore an idea: it might work, it might just work. "I have an idea, Sicinnus. Will you back me on this?"

Theodore had sent Sicinnus on a mission when Andrew, the son of Lysimachus, approached. They were not friends, for Theodore had him ostracized. "The enemy surrounds us!" announced Andrew. "Thank you for coming at a time like this," Theodore said apologetically.

"What are your plans? Asked Andrew. He was a nobleman and admired by his countrymen and would have more influence on them than Theodore.

"If you can round up the generals and trierarchs and incite them to battle, we can fight the Persians in the shallow and narrow strait of Salamis," Theodore said, looking up to see Panaetius approaching in a Tenian trireme, a deserter of the Persian Navy. "You are surrounded, and there is no way out," announced

Panaetius. "Confrontation with courage is the only solution."

The Persians had moved into position overnight. Their fleet has been reduced to half on two separate sea storms. Some had fled, but the majority were lost at sea. The Shah was oblivious to the marshaling of natural threats against him. The winds and the ocean had been punished with three hundred lashes for destroying two army bridges. But the sea had retaliated by sending gale winds that destroyed two ships for every lash. The monstrous storms swallowed many ships carrying grain and rations for the soldiers.

Commander Demaratus, a Greek from Sparta who was in the Navy of King Dawit, approached the head commanders. He had seen messages left by Theodore. "We should send a part of the fleet to the island of Cythera and use it as a base to attack the Peloponnese."

Artabanus did not trust Demaratus. Greeks were known to be double-crossers, switching sides in the middle of the battle. Why was he suggesting the fleet be divided? Was this a ploy to give his countrymen an advantage over a smaller fleet? The Greeks had already tried to influence the Ionians in the north to turn against the Persians and join them in the battle for democracy. "The fleet should not be divided," replied Artabanus. "It would put us at a disadvantage. We have already lost six hundred ships to storms and are not taking a chance," he looked at King Dawit for confirmation.

"Mardonius, consult with the other Naval Commanders for their opinions since they are engaging in the sea battle with their entire forces," recommended King Dawit.

The Commanders gathered to discuss the matter, and King Dawit listened to their opinions. The majority agreed that the fleet should not be divided, except for Artemisia, who had just joined them.

The female Admiral was a half-sister of Queen Zenia. She was given in marriage to her late husband, King of Caria, by the late King Darius to ally with the two countries. She arrived with a message for the King. "My sister Zenia is not in the land of the Hellenes. The Royal lady suffered a violent attack after the Battle of Babylon and is vegetated." Artemisia was the Queen of Caria. Her fleet was caught in the gale winds, and she had lost three ships during her voyage. The image of her crew drowning was still vivid in her mind.

King Dawit was bittersweet at this report; he wanted to go to Zenia but was already in place to subjugate the Hellenes. The other commanders already suspected that the Greeks had not taken the Queen, for everyone they questioned did not know what they were talking about.

"May I speak my opinion?" asked Artemisa, following a long silence. "All we have to do is to wait, your Highness."

"Wait," resounded King Dawit, still shocked by the news. The laughter and chatter in the room got loud. The other commanders thought it was ludicrous to sit and wait.

"Yes, wait," Artemisia continued, ignoring the comments from the men around her. "The Greeks do not have enough resources to hold them for the winter months and would surrender. I am uncomfortable engaging in a battle at sea, for many of our men are not great swimmers and are unfamiliar with the narrowing channels of the strait."

"What speak thy, woman!" said Mardonius. "Our resources have been diminished with the storms, and time we have not for the Greeks to surrender. We will not last through the winter months, much less fight without supplies. We must not tarry."

Some commanders wanted the battle to end, especially now that they knew Zenia was not in the islands. They were anxious to return home to their families and did not want to be on the Aegean Island during winter. The winter months were horrible, with storms that formed in the Mediterranean and northerly winds reaching gale forces of 93 km. None would survive.

"Mardonius is correct, for much supply and grain has been lost at sea. Autumn approaches, giving way to winter upon us. The supply routes have become more difficult to maintain, and waiting could be long," said the King. He was also anxious to end the battle with the news of Zenia. "The fleet has been reduced, but our numbers are still superior to the Greeks," continued the Shah, hopeful.

"But the Greeks have hemmed themselves in and confined themselves to the land. There is not much they can do; they are surrounded by sea and land. There are other routes to infiltrate the Peloponnese," reasoned Artemisia.

The commanders were in a significant dispute when a messenger arrived—a slave in a small boat with a message for the Shah. A tall Persian man with thick white hair and droopy eyes prostrated before the King. "I have a message from the General of the Athenians," he announced. "The Athenian general elects the King's cause and is the first to announce to him that the Hellenes are trying to sail away." King Dawit sat on his golden throne and looked suspiciously at the messenger but welcomed a peaceful solution.

"He bids you not to suffer them to escape, but while they are in confusion and separated from their infantry to set upon them and destroy their naval power," continued the messenger. "The Greeks could not govern themselves and needed a king to rule over them. The Shah can achieve a brilliant coup if he doesn't stand and watch them run. The General is ready to discuss peaceful negotiations and bring this battle to an end. You can strike fast and hard at the fleet departing north of the Bay of Eleusis and will win."

"I believe not what the messenger is saying," said Artemisia. "Greeks are combative and do not give up easily; they will die before surrendering their freedoms."

"The Greeks are a disorganized people, changing their disposition. I am also suspicious of this message," said Gabe, taking out his whip. He was quiet unless he had something important to say, but this hoaxer had to be disciplined for trying to wink-hook the King. "Why are you deceiving the Shah?" he asked, whipping the messenger.

"Please do not whip me, for I swear by the gods that this is the truth, and the Shah must act if he is to gain control over the Hellenes," cried Sicinnus in agony, fearing he would be frayed alive.

"I do not know what to think of this," Mardonius said doubtfully. He knew the Greeks to be fabricators of fables, always striving with each other and no better with others.

"This is perfect," said Demaratus. He knew this was a huge mistake, for General Theodore was known to be quick-witted. But King Dawit was confident of victory, for his fleet vastly outnumbered the Greeks, and the foot soldiers were already on the mainland.

"I trust not the messenger," said Mardonius, his eyebrows creasing. Meanwhile, Gabe continued whipping the poor slave. No one cared for his cries.

King Dawit always preferred a peaceful disposition of conquest. It would give him victory if he could end the battle in peace while advancing to the city-states. "Take the messenger and sacrifice him," ordered the King. Poor Sicinnus feared this would happen. He was put on a stake and burned alive; his cries echoed over the fresh breeze from the sea to the ears of General Theodore and the Admirals.

"The barbarians have no compassion," said Theodore to the Admirals after the cries died. "Listen and hear how they treat one of their own. What will you do, my brothers, when they come for you?" When he said this, a white owl flew over him, inspiring the men to stand in strength and courage.

"We have three hundred and twenty fighting ships," said Andrew excitedly. "We can have a one-hundred-and-eighty-man crew, eighteen hoplites, four archers, and the remaining men at arms. We will fight ramming, disabling, and jumping on their ships to fight hand-to-hand in the formation of hoplites. The barbarians are poor swimmers. Throw them to the harem of the sirens for victory."

"We will start the formation at the sound of flutes and lyres. Crush the enemy, and their bodies will drift to the shore," cried another Admiral. The men erupted in cheers of mania and frenzy that boomed in the full moonlight.

"The battle cries will be heard from sea to shining armor," exhorted Theodore; "democracy will prevail, and the rest goes to Hades."

"Sacrifice the beautiful prisoners. Sacrifice the adorned princes with raiment and gold to Dionysus

Carnivorous. Offer prayers of supplications for Hellenes' victory!" cried Seer.

"Sacrifice?" cried out Theodore, in unbelief and horrified. "That's monstrous!" he exclaimed.

"SACRIFICE, SACRIFICE!" cried the men in unison. Theodore could not believe his ears, but if that's what the troops wanted, then that's what they would get.

"Bring the three princes," cried the Seer, his fanatical light blue eyes in flames. "We will consecrate and sacrifice the youths as an offering to Dionysus Carnivorous with prayers and supplications for victory over the barbarians!" Usually, the Olympian god of wine, madness, and wild frenzy was offered sacred animals, panthers, tigers, bulls, or serpents, but humans? That was a new one for Theodore.

The three boys, members of the royal family, were dragged to the altar as the Seer commanded and sacrificed, sending up a sweet, glaring offering flame to the god of wine, madness, and wild frenzy. Theodore could feel the changing winds approaching the shores. *Lee shore winds?* He thought, making a mental note to himself. The vessels must be anchored in a safer spot and wait out the treacherous winds in shallow coastal waters. Maneuvering was usually impaired during this sea condition; waves got steeper, and objects became obscured, but he was confident that his crew knew how to steer toward the wind and luff the sails for the airflow of the wind to push toward land.

CHAPTER TWENTY-NINE

THE DEFEAT

O n the morning of September 30, the Persians entered the straits and bay of Salamis. They navigated through very narrow points between the shores of Attica and Psyttaleia. A large shoal broke the path, creating dangerous and serious obstructions to naval movement, even during the day.

King Dawit did not dismiss the possibility that Theodore was defecting and dispatched ships to the Straits of Salamis to block both entrances. The commanders were threatened with death if the Greeks escaped the blockade. On rough Silenian rocks on the hill of Salamis stood Artembares, leader of ten thousand calvary, projecting into the bay. They aimed to slaughter the Greeks who might be driven ashore in the battle.

It was a beautiful, clear, and bright day. The King could see clearly. The calm waters concealed the inhospitable coast of the mainland of Attica. King Dawit had a grandstand view from his golden throne above the Phanodemus and the Hercacleium horns. Two scribes stood behind him, ready to detail the battle event. On his right-hand side was Gabe, his bodyguard. The island of Psyttaleia was the central point in the battle.

On the western wing, the Phoenicians faced the Athenians, and the Ionians faced the Spartans. On the left flank were the Carians and Dorians. Behind the main Greek line, the Aegina contingent and some Athenian ships waited in reserve. The Corinthians were stationed west of the battle line, protecting the passage to Eleusis. The Cyprians, Cilicians, and Hellespoinines stay back to the south, guarding the exit to Piraeus. The Egyptian fleet sealed off the straits between Salamis and Megara to engage any Greek ships breaking off the main fleet.

From the Shah's view, he could see the Hellespont entirely covered by his ships and the coast plains overrun by his soldiers. He felt a deep sense of satisfaction and started weeping.

"Why weep you so suddenly," asked Gabe, concerned for the King.

Look at all my soldiers. I feel compassion for them," he cried. "Short is the sum total of their life. None of them will be alive in a hundred years."

The Persian ships, three in line, stood opposite the Greeks, extending from the Gulf of Eleusis's entrance almost to the Piraeus's entrance. The main movement was to cut off the escape of the Greeks from Salamis.

The Navy trireme were wooden warships, light, streamlined, and maneuverable to those who knew. They were powered by one hundred and seventy oarsmen split in three ranks down each side of the ship. They could accelerate, brake, and zigzag, turning 360 degrees in just two ship's lengths. Good sea captains could place the vessel to the best advantage and employ principal naval warfare strategies. The primary strategy was to ram the enemy, making full use of the bronze ram fitted to the vessel's prow. They carried a small complement of soldiers, fourteen combatants, and 30 Medes armed with bows, spears, and swords. The Greek vessels had at least ten hoplites and four archers. At close quarters, the enemy would board the enemy vessel for hand-to-hand fighting.

The vessels operated well in calm sea, with waves less than 1 mile high. But when the ocean was unstable, the water would enter via the oar ports and flood the ship. They had to stay close to the shore, and the light wood had to be beached so as not to become water-logged, which would reduce their speed and performance. There was little space on board for provision and no sleeping quarters for the crew. The warriors had to land each night to rest.

The commanders led from the front with their ship at the heart of the battle. Maneuvers could be signaled to other vessels in the fleet using flags and trumpeters. Once the battle was in full force, the conflict became a case of single ship against a single opponent. To do this, they had to cross the enemy line, smash through gaps in the enemy line, and attack from their rear flank. These moves were to get one's ship in a position to ram the weakest point of the enemy- the side or stern quarter. The aim was to puncture a hole in the enemy vessel or break enough of their oars to disable the ship. Damaging one's oars was possible, but to avoid this. The crew were drilled to withdraw in seconds, usually on one side while the other maintained the vessel's momentum. These defense tactics enabled the commander to ensure that his flanks were closed off by shallows or coastline and that his crew was drilled to maintain close. In open water, the ships could not organize in a defensive circle or an arch with larger fleets with prows pointing outward.

The Greeks prepared their vessels at several bays on the island of Salamis from Cynosoura to Paloukia. These islands had been evacuated. Greek ships quietly concealed between the two passes. Theodore had harangued the Greek crews on the shore at daybreak across the bay. Several ships started to sail when the morning sea breeze began to blow.

The Shah could see Greek ships as though they were fleeing north to the Bay of Eleusis when suddenly he heard the sound of lyres and lutes as the Greek ships turned around chanting war songs loudly that echoed from the rocky hills of Salamis. They were not fleeing; they were setting up their formation. The barbarians were seized with terror. Persians eagerly pushed forward to cut the Greeks in the gap when the Aeginetan and Megarian appeared from their hiding on the left.

Gabe saw a bright light blazed out from Eleusis. He heard echoes over the Thracian Plain riding the waves of the sea; he felt the rushing winds. A woman's hand rose from the sea with a clenched sword and a crown on its tip. For the first time in his life, he was frightened. King Dawit heard the echoes and the winds but felt his crown lifted from his head by an invisible force.

The morning swells had begun, and the Phoenician ships were in the tightest corner of the straits with little room to move when they heard the sound of a trumpet from afar, and the cries of the Greeks followed:

CHILDREN OF GREEKS ARISE, ARISE

FREE YOUR COUNTRY,

FREE YOUR CHILDREN,

FREE YOUR WIVES,

FREE THE SHRINES OF THE FATHERS,

FREE THE GODS,

AND THE TOMBS OF YOUR ANCESTORS!

NOW, WE FIGHT FOR ALL,

NOW, WE FIGHT FOR FREEDOM.

Admiral Andrew dashed forward with his ship before the blockage, engaging a Persian ship. The two ships became so entangled that they could not be separated, beginning the battle. The Ionian ships behind the Phoenician ships crushed into them in the narrow path. This crucially weakened the Persian fleet, and fighting was confused; encounters were mainly between individual ships. The Persians advanced, becoming more closely packed as they aligned themselves with the enemy's narrower point. The Greek ships were slower, but the Persian rowers were tired from the night's journey. There was not a moment of delay as the Greeks started to target and crush figureheads. At the first stream, the Persian fleet held its own, but in the cramped conditions of the Straits, the great Persian numbers were a hindrance. Ariabignes, a brother of King Dawit, a mighty warrior and archer, was left open, and two Greek ships encircled him, killing him and his crew. When his ships were demolished, the Persian ships were put to flight, and most of them were destroyed, for those behind them strived to push forward. A multitude of vessels was crowded in the narrows, so they could not help each other; the brazen beaks of their ships struck them, their armament of oars crushed while the Grecian ships followed right-wing, move on through the Persian lines curving around to surround them in a diekplous formation, tight ships facing their enemy. The Greek ships had more space to maneuver and pick off the closely packed vessels that could not retreat, encircling the Persians, striking the hulls of the boats, and turning them upside down. Panic cries of men filled the air. The Greeks fought in good order, while the Persians did not keep their line. Another Persian Admiral was targeted by the Aeginetans and killed. When the Greek ships were destroyed, they could swim to the shore, but the Persians suffered many casualties. The glimpse of the sea was brimming with wrecked ships and dead men. When the barbarians sailed towards Phalerum, the Aeginetans posted themselves in the channel and did notable deeds. In the tumult of the battle, the Athenians disabled the Persian ships, which either made resistance or took to flight. At the same time, the Aeginetans dealt with those who succeeded in passing the straits, and when any escaped the Athenians, they fell into the hands of the Aeginetans. The winds washed the shores, reefs, and sea of human remains.

King Dawit could hardly believe his eyes as the disaster unfolded. He had been deceived and should have listened to Artemisa, who fought bravely, and unafraid, ramming ships left and right.

The Greeks struck and split over the sea with broken oars and fragments of wreckage at the Persians, who were like fishes caught in a net, overboard.

The wails of the Shah pierced through the swelling waves as he witnessed the disaster. He rented his royal robes and tore his hair and beard. The shrill screams mounted even unto the seventh sphere, alarming the infantry to retreat. Tears watered the ground, blinding his eyes with weeping and lamentation. The outcome was unexpected. It was a defeat for the Great King, who sat on a golden throne and ruled with an iron fist.

The groaning, wailing, and shrieking spread over the sea until the eye of dark bade it to cease, and the full moon showed its face. The sea was blood as the winds moved around to the north, mainly washing Persian corpses on the shore of Salamis.

It was a dark and anxious time for King Dawit. When he began evacuating Attica, he had difficulty preparing to march to Boeotia. But he had to move. Gabe would carry him if necessary. If the Hellespont was destroyed, the King's escape route and army would be cut off in hostile territory. The defeat was terrible, but Gabe was concerned for the safety of the King. It was his job to ensure the King was preserved.

The Persian ships retreated to Asia Minor, and the Greeks transferred the hoplite force to Salamis over the mainland to fight the Persian land forces.

Mardonius was determined to remain on the land and continue with the land campaign. "Leave me with an army of 300,000 chosen men to undertake the conquest of Greece," he pleaded with King Dawit. The Persian position was still strong despite the defeat; much of Greece was controlled, and their large land was intact. After a series of political discussions, it became clear that the Persians would not gain victory on land through diplomacy. "Enough is enough," said Gabe to the disputing commanders. Mardonius wanted to continue in the battle, but Artemisia also had enough. "Abort the land campaign and retreat the army to Thessaly for the winter," Artemisia said to the King. The King did not want Greece to know he was retreating and feared the Greeks would destroy the Hellespont bridges and they would be stranded in Greece without provision for his warriors.

Theodore urged the Peloponnesian leaders to destroy the bridge of Hellespont, but the other Admirals opposed this vigorously. "Make their escape as easy as possible, for I want them off our borders," said Edward.

By late Winter, King Dawit had retreated with the bulk of his army, reached Abydos, and boarded a ship from Eion on the Strydom and back to Asia.

When the news arrived in Susa, there was much weeping. Many went out into the streets in sackcloth and ashes, for great was the lost. Amara heard the news of morn and cried, for she knew not if Todd had survived the carnage.

CHAPTER THIRTY

THE PRICE

T he tears of frankincense perfumed the air. Queen Zenia could see a three-tiered fountain. The water flowed endlessly with leaping fishes. Beautiful white flowers covered the base, reminding her of lotus flowers. Life was a set of circumstances that leaped out of the wilderness, and one had to surrender to the flow. She had to let go of attachments, as told by the Magi. Beyond the intricacies and nuances of everyday life danced a cosmic energy with a rhythm that moved thoughts and emotions in the roles played in society. Zenia had always been an external being, interconnected with others. Her mind was filled with a deep sense of peace and unity that belonged to her, no matter what the day brought. She saw a servant girl carrying a beautiful male child. Her child, she was told, was a gift from God.

Only her eyes adored him, for she had no consciousness of arms to hold him nor legs to carry him around the garden. One day, she will be whole again; at least, that's what her caregivers told her, but no one could foresee when or how. She had become a wretched woman, but her love was not broken, for love could not be broken; it just strengthens one. Zenia's condition was not a punishment sent by God but a hindrance by cruel humans.

A young maiden approached Zenia. "My Lady, it is time to soak in the hot springs." Three servant girls lifted her to a light four-wheeled horse chariot and took her to the spring. Another servant disrobed her, and they gently placed her in the hot water from the earth's core. Zenia could not feel anything but welcomed the soak. "The healing waters will ease the phantom pain and comfort your mind," said one of the servants. Afterward, a healer would massage her limbs and spine with frankincense oil to strengthen them. In the afternoon, the child was brought to her, and even though she could not embrace him, her sparkling eyes did. It was unsettling for her the experience of being trapped in a body between parts with standard functions and those that were not normal. The broken nerves and trauma to her head were ever-present in her daily life—burning and prickly sensations. She could still run, hunt, fight, and rule in her dreams at night, but others carried and cared for her in the daytime. It had been a surreal experience for her. The Magi thought her body was just in shock. Although Zenia had repeatedly told him he should not carry the burden, he felt responsible for what happened.

"How long have my limbs been unconscious?" she asked the servant girl, dressed in white linen. "My Lady, thou are much concerned with time. It has been forty lunar months. Your injuries threatened your life, and for many months, you were not able to speak, and your mind did not remember. The evil man wanted to destroy you, but the gods protected you."

"Tell me again what happened," Queen Zenia asked. It was not the first time she had been told, but she wanted to hear it again and again, for each time she heard it, a new revelation was revealed to her.

"It was after you, my Lady, had bravery destroyed the Arabic cohorts who came to destroy Babylon. An evil man was concealed in the hollow body of Marduk. He killed Gaia, the High Priest, then went to your chambers to destroy you. You were putting Iskandar to rest when the wicked man tried to slay you. Alarmed by the child's cries, Naomi entered your chamber and was slewed by the man. The Magi was near, and he entered the room. The man stood over you to decapitate you when the Magi slewed him. Fearing for your life and the life of your child, he brought you here to restore your health."

Zenia could remember some of what had happened, but only some things. "Why did the wicked man come to inflict punishment upon me? Was he a known enemy in Babylon?" she inquired.

"The Magi learned that Ahmed Abdul was offered a large amount of gold to carry out the mischief," answered the servant. Zenia wanted to know if they knew who sent him, but she already knew the answer: Mother Queen, an intelligent, jealous, and demented woman who exerted power over her son, the King. Zenia swore to herself that someday, and not too far in the future, Mother Queen would pay for her evil deeds.

The Murashu Family, relatives of the Magi, had seen the misfortune that had come to Zenia, for she suffered loss and deprivation. They owned large land of Boswellia Trees in the Arabian Peninsula. The trees were sparsely grown in forests on rocks and sand in the southern tip of Arabian, where Monsoon water mountains met the desert. The Magi used the light resin that leaked as tears from the tree's bark to make ointments, salves, and oils. The oils were used to massage Zenia in the mornings. In the afternoons, she was rubbed with myrrh; in the evening, a combination of both oils was used. Weekly, a series of caravans traveled through hostile Arabia to bring the oils from Mesopotamia, Tigris, and Euphrates Rivers to the encampment.

That morning, the Magi had arrived from a trip to Magnesia, Anatolia. He brought magnetite rocks called lodestones. These rocks attached metal to themselves or magnetized other rocks. He had news of the defeated Persians in the Aegean Islands but would not concern Zenia with that. Her memory of what had happened was still vague.

As soon as he arrived, he went to see Zenia. "It was a favorable trip, and I discovered magnetite crystals," he said cheerfully. "These crystals will be used to design a healing chamber. I must find the exact point to build a dome." Zenia was thrilled at the news, even though she could not understand what he was saying.

The following day, the Magi evaluated the earth, looking for something. When he found what he was looking for, he put a marker on the ground and commissioned workers to build a miniature ziggurat with magnetite crystals. According to his reference book of symbols and patterns, the dome was designed. It took months, after it was completed, he enlisted musicians with gongs, didgeridos, and flutes to play harmonic sounds. "What mysteries are you doing?" asked Zenia. "I am not sure how the mystery works, but the vibrations of the instruments cause the body to oscillate, which could promote healing." That was terrific news. At that time, Iskandar crawled into the dome, he was an adorable cherub with golden hair, and distinguished eyes. The baby jumped on his mother's lap, smothering her with hugs and kisses. One day, her son will be the King.

After the Battle of Salamis, the demoralized King Dawit could not be comforted. His heart yearned for Zenia, and he did not know where she was. The desire for revenge and punishment carried him away. His grief was profound, for he had lost four brothers and three nephews. Mother Queen tried to induce him with the harem, but even that did not help with the spell of misfortune that had come upon him. He did not understand how it came upon him and believed Ahura Mazda had forsaken him.

He sometimes was frightened that he could not sleep by day or night with disturbing dreams and grew weaker, not having enough food and drink. It was not the same when he sat on his royal throne with robes of interwoven gold and precious stones. Soured by his failure, he stayed in Sardis another year before he retired to Susa. *"For the misfortunes that befall us and the illnesses that harass us make even a short life seem long. And so, because life is a hardship, death proves to be a human being's most welcome escape, and the God, who gives us merely a taste of sweetness in life, is revealed to be a jealous deity."*

Daniel completed his writings and placed the scroll in a limestone cave near Khirbet Qumran on the northwestern shores of the Dead Sea.

THE END

The earth was ever thirsty for more blood. The fire was ever ready to burn and consume. The winds were ready to scatter and stir, while the bottomless ocean was never full. All creation mourned as if in labor pain, even the King, crushed in spirit.

The search for Queen Zenia in Greece was a disaster. King Dawit could not understand why Mother Queen had suspected the Hellenes, but it motivated him to move forward with the plans to subjugate the Greeks and rescue the Queen. No one suspected Mother Queen was responsible for the destruction that came upon Babylon and the missing Queen and her child, except her brother, Artabanus. Everything had worked against the King, and Artabanus believed Ahura Mazda did not favor the battle for several reasons. First, it was a deception, and second, King Dawit offered sacrifices to daevas before the battle, stirring up spirits from the dark and followers of the Lie that worked against him. The pride of the King expected the elements to obey him. Only God had that power, and although King Dawit was supposed to be both man and God, he was not above the Creator.

The Shah realized his mistakes after the Battle of Salamis. He needed to get his army out of Greece for the Winter months. Gabe, his bodyguard, also feared the Hellespont bridge would be destroyed and the King would be trapped in Greece. Thoughts of retreat did not settle well for King Dawit, but he had to return to Asia. He realized invading by sea on a perilous coast without ports was unbridled arrogance. Of all the armies that set out, only a few had survived. There were repercussions after the war. King Dawit had lost three brothers and three nephews, all royal princes. Artabanus' son, Todd, had vanished when Athens was burned. The exact number of deaths, vessels, and supplies were unknown. The defeat was terrible, but the danger was the empire collapsing if the King did not return.

Mardonius wanted to continue the land campaigns, but the King retreated him to Thessaly for the Winter. 'They who fight and retreat with their lives will fight again another season,' he said to Mandonius. The King promoted him to the Satrap of Greece and offered 300,000 soldiers and provisions to lead the next campaign to Greece in the spring.

Artemisia left at night with the remaining navy vessels shortly after the battle of Salamis. She did not want to disclose details regarding her sister, Queen Zenia, when King Dawit asked about her location. "I know not where the Queen is, but those caring for her fear a threat still exists." She advised the King to reassess future naval battles, for the Persian admirals lacked navigational skills in perilous waters.

The north wind was behind the Persians as they marched from Thessaly to Hellespont. It was a forty-day journey. Retreat plans were shattered, and there was insufficient food and water to feed the large army. Many of the warriors died from diseases and bad water. Others drowned during the crossing of the frozen River Strymon that cracked under the heavyweight. When the troops arrived at Abdera, the King took a brief respite, where some warriors gorged themselves to death. The Shah stayed in Sardis for a year before returning to Susa. He was not enthusiastic about going home to face the consequences of his actions. He agreed with Gabe that he needed to restore his confidence to maintain the solidity of his kingdom.

The City of Babylon and the Temple of Marduk were restored. Another High Priest was assigned to replace Gaia, and the city reverted back to King Dawit. Norman continued administrating the day-to-day operations of Zenia's estates. He never did recover from the death of his wife, Naomi.

Lydia and the cavalry of women had helped Gaspar the Magi during the mayhem in Babylon and helped move Queen Zenia from the city, ensuring her safety. They were hired to deliver frankincense, myrrh, and other oils to the Magi for the Queen's medical treatments.

Mother Queen continued to maintain the harem under the eyes of Haggai, waiting for the return of her son. She ensured the young girls completed their rituals to be deflowered when her son returned to Susa. Her health was failing, and the lump on her breast was growing again. Dr. Democedes, her physician, did not return from Greece, and the healers in Susa did not know how to deal with her illness. Rose stayed close to her like an obedient and faithful hound, making her comfortable, especially during her moments of anxiety, depression, anger, and uncertainty about the future. She did not feel any remorse for what she did to Zenia. In her mind, she had gotten rid of the daevas from Babylon.

Amara was overwhelmed with grief. Todd was reported missing in action. The initial shock of the news made her numb as she watched life unfold like a repeated nightmare. The damsel wondered what she had done wrong and why she was being punished. In her private thoughts, she held animosity toward her Uncle Kaleb for bringing her to the harem. Her aunt Martha was not allowed to visit her, and she yearned to go home. Amara had difficulty sleeping at night, and it was hard to focus during the day. It was difficult for her to accept Todd was dead and had hope that he was still alive. At times, she would get angry at Todd for leaving her, but deep down inside, she knew it would have been different under different circumstances. The little gold ring on her finger reminded her of the love that was and could have been. Vanessa, her helpmate, continued to comfort her during the long hours of weeping with songs and stories, lifting her dying spirit. Amara's biggest fear was the return of King Dawit, for upon his arrival, she would be presented for deflowering.

Uncle Kaleb did not feel any remorse for putting Amara in a harem. He was confident that she would rise to be the Queen of Persia. Mother Queen had promoted him to a high advisor for saving her life, and he was living a distinguished lifestyle. Amara will someday realize all he has done for her and thank him for it. The little dowry her father left will not matter, for she will have plenty. His wife, Martha, also resented him. Amara was her niece, the daughter of her brother. Kaleb was considered her legal guardian, but he was not a blood relative. Behind the scenes, there was tension building that Kaleb knew nothing about, but there was a vizier, close to the Mother Queen, who plotted against him.

Amber, the tiger, slowly recovered from her injuries and was released back to the royal jungle. Her tormentors were still fresh in her mind.

In a grave, they laid thee, the armies of Spartans, who slashed through the enemy in the realm of death.

The Greeks mourned the death of King Leonidas and three hundred heroic men who made their last stand defending the pass of Thermopylae. King Leonidas left behind his wife, Gorgo, and son, Pleistarchus, a young boy. Gorgo recovered her husband's decapitated body and had it buried in a tomb north of Agora.

The three hundred warriors also left behind an heir to carry out their name, a prerequisite before they joined the suicide mission. They were buried on a hill called Kolonos. Over the stones of the heroes was written, "Go, stranger, and tell the Lacedaemonians that we lie here in obedience to their laws."

King Leonidas' brother Pausanias succeeded him to the throne until his son was of age. The victory of the Greeks did not end Persia's desire to conquer them. The city-states still had animosity but learned to work together for common purposes. The leaders formed a more permanent alliance among themselves.

When King Dawit arrived at Thessaly, a herald arrived from the Spartan's state, commanding he compensates them for the death of King Leonidas and the three hundred men. After a long pause, the Shah burst out laughing. "All right," he said, pointing at Mardonius next to him. "Here's Mardonius; he'll pay them what they deserve."

General Theodore continued his ambitious politics. Many leaders were angry after he scavenged among the bodies of dead Persian warriors, seeking gold and silver to re-fortify Athen. Sparta had always opposed General Theodore for his arrogance and democratic reforms. This stirred up a lot of animosity between the two dominant states, and the winds of quarrel continued to blow as they prepared for another battle in the Spring.

King Dawit never ceased to stop yearning for Queen Zenia. He thought their story was not over, and someday in the future, their worlds would intertwine, and once again, they would dine and wine to the nectar of divine love.

Queen Zenia lived in a protected encampment, recovering from paralysis. The baby was a toddler, learning to walk and talk. He was a handsome, moon-faced child, perfect in form, with the heart of a lion and distinguished eyes.

AFTERWORD

I began writing Defiant Throne around 2022, near the end of COVID-19. The lockdown and isolation afforded me time to seek a deeper understanding of government officials and their societal roles. I did a lot of reading and had just completed studying the book of Esther in the Bible. It was not the first time I had read the book, but the first time I read it critically. The book is about a young Hebrew maiden who replaces the Queen of Persia and stops the genocide of her people. Still, I had questions as to what was really going on. What happened to Vashi (Zenia) after she was banished from the presence of her husband, the King? Was there an alimony allowance for her? How did it work in those days? Did women have rights; was there civil unrest?

These questions prompted me to do intense research in the world of 5 B.C. The Zeitgeist continues to march through time and space and only leaves fragments of history for us to glean. I am thankful for all those who contributed to the research that helped build the storyline. I will be the first to say I knew nothing about the Achaemenid Empire when I started writing the book, but I became excited when I linked it to the Esther story. I launched a Google search of the Persian Empire and found a large manuscript from the University of Chicago. This led to deeper research into the time customs, habits, and situations that led me to the Greco-Persian Wars. My life has never been the same. I wanted to link all the rich information into my storyline.

The story was built on research premises and a vivid imagination.

The book of Esther opens with a banquet. The Mighty Shah of the Achaemenid Empire was a man who was 8 feet tall, ruler of a vast empire, and the wealthiest man in the world. The grand fest was for his military generals and government officials in preparation for a campaign to Greece. The King was married to the most beautiful woman in the entire dynasty. Her name was Vashi. For some unknown reason, the men broke into a discussion as to who was the most beautiful and fairest of the women. The King was incredibly proud of his wife and spoke highly of her. The generals requested to see her. The Shah, who was light with wine, sent an escort to get her. When the messenger arrived to escort Vashi to the banquet, naked, wearing only the crown, the righteous Queen refused. Everyone knew what kind of woman would be paraded naked before the King and his drunken warriors. She refused to embarrass her husband and demean herself.

The courts dismissed the poor Queen. What was a woman to do? Where does she go, who would go with her, how will she travel, could she travel, or were there laws that prohibited women from going in public? The future of the young Queen was uncertain. To top it off, a line of beautiful women were lined up to take her place; how would that feel?

My investigation started with Vashi (Zenia), the central character of my story. Who was Vashi? Where did she come from? Who were the parents? How did she become the wife of King Xerxes? The information I found was very concerning. Historically, Vashi has been portrayed as an evil woman by Hebrew writers. It was said she stripped Jewish women naked and ordered them to perform work on the Sabbath. This was the King's way of punishing her. "Really, I asked?" What were Hebrews doing in Susa? The

Sabbath was a day of rest commanded by God in the Book of Exodus, but Vashi was Babylonian, a Chaldean, and this incident took place in Susa. They did not follow the customs of the Torah; not even Mordecai seemed to follow the teachings. He did not appear to follow the traditions; he subjected his niece Esther to a harem. The Prophet Ezra disapproved of interracial marriages and had all Hebrew men put away their non-Hebrew wives, so why was Mordecai joining his niece, a decedent of King Saul, to be married to a Zoroastrian King? I understood that the Great King Cyrus had allowed the Hebrews to return to Jerusalem, so what was Mordecai doing in Susa?

There is a lot of controversy regarding the Book of Esther, my favorite book in the Bible, and I needed to sort through all the misinformation and half-truths. According to the research, Martin Luther believed the book should have been excluded from the canon because it was Judaistic and did not mention God.

It would be an injustice if I did not venture into Greek History, their lifestyles, and their ways of life. I took a deep dive into Plutarch -the lives of the Noble Grecians and Romans to give actual characteristics to my Greek generals. I have always enjoyed Greek classics:

The Histories by Herodotus, Plato, Aristotle, Homer, The Iliad, and, of course, the Odyssey, my all-time favorite.

Information on the customs and habits of the Greek ladies was scarce. Greek women were administrators in their homes and raised children. However, my focus was on the harem in Persia, where the women were being prepared for the beauty contest to replace the Queen. There was a plethora of information regarding the Olympics and the significance of the games.

The storyline has three battles: one in the desert, one on land, and the last at sea, and the elements that stir up when life is hectic and challenging. The Battle of Thermopylae and the Battle of Salamis are historically documented, and plenty of information exists.

The language utilized was a combination of dialects that were probably used in those days. I ask for forgiveness from the expert linguists. The Persians and the Greeks spoke poetically, using figurative language and imagery. I tried to mimic the language to the best of my ability.

There are many controversies regarding the historical accuracy of Herodotus, who seemed to favor the Greek narrative, and Josephus, who favored the narrative of Israel. The history of the Achaemenid dynasty mainly consists of reports from Herodotus, Thucydides, and Xenophanes.

The Achaemenid Empire was an advanced society with written laws, large libraries, and literature, but today, only fragments of stone tablets remain of their history. Where did all the history disappear? The oldest text from Persian is the Gathas, a short hymn book written in an archaic form of an old Iranian language called Avestan, the holy book of Zoroastrianism.

Zoroastrianism is one of the oldest and first religions to practice monotheism, the one God. The movement was established by the Prophet Zoroaster, who claimed to have transmitted God's messages, challenging other existing religious traditions. The teaching impacted Plato, Pythagoras, and the Abrahamic religions, which branched into Judaism, Christianity, and Islam.

I was delighted when I discovered the Epic of Gilgamesh, composed by a scribe named Sin-lieu-running during the Middle Babylonian Period.

The journey was refreshing and enjoyable. I learned the hardest lesson for a "novice writer," perseverance. There were many times I wanted to quit. It was a difficult time for me as the aftermath of COVID-19 started unveiling. I lost my best friend Kim to COVID. I lost my sister to breast cancer. My husband was hospitalized with a pulmonary embolism. My mother was also hospitalized with hyperglycemia. The writing journey was on a perilous road, heading in the same direction in which many of my writings have landed: nowhere. This time, though, I continued to push through in the middle of the storms and redirected my path like a good sea captain.

There was a time of soul-searching, and I questioned my motive for writing the book. This is not a religious book, but it brings back the essence of the religious institutions that were at play during that time. I myself am a practicing Christian, and I love Jesus. However, this story was 'Before Christ.' At the time, the walls of Jerusalem were still not built, and the people were still bickering among themselves over land.

My aha moment was when I realized, "Generations have come, and generations have gone, but nothing has changed, has it? There is still food scarcity, emergency catastrophic events, pestilences, discrimination, wars, and more rumors of wars. Men continue to lord over others as the earth continues to open its mouth and swallow the blood of men.

The Zeitgeist of time marches away

awake, awake, and learn his ways

Ideas, beliefs, and religions change

As men live in fire and flames

Striving, lying, and conniving,

Climates and pestilences are the same

They just take a different name

As men kill each other for fame

The heart of men is still not tame

They just take on a new name

While men bare no shame

Who takes the blame?

As Zeitgeist walks the pane

The womb of women

Moan in pain.